BEYOND
BIDEN

BEYOND BIDEN

Rebuilding the America We Love

NEWT GINGRICH

CENTER
STREET

NEW YORK   NASHVILLE

Center Street
Hachette Book Group
1290 Avenue of the Americas, New York, NY 10104
centerstreet.com
twitter.com/centerstreet

First Edition: November 2021

Center Street is a division of Hachette Book Group, Inc.
The Center Street name and logo are trademarks of Hachette Book Group, Inc.

The publisher is not responsible for websites (or their content)
that are not owned by the publisher.

The Hachette Speakers Bureau provides a wide range of authors for speaking events. To find out more, go to www.hachettespeakersbureau.com or call (866) 376-6591.

Print book interior design by Timothy Shaner

Library of Congress Cataloging-in-Publication Data has been applied for.

ISBNs: 978-1-5460-0025-9 (hardcover), 978-1-5460-0026-6 (ebook)

Printed in the United States of America
LSC-H
Printing 2, 2021

Beyond Biden is dedicated to the millions of Americans who suffered, endured, and prevailed throughout the COVID-19 pandemic. It was their courage and patriotism that carried our country through one of the worst crises in our nation's history. Because of their triumph, we look forward to an exciting and prosperous future.

CONTENTS

CONTENTS

CONTENTS

BEYOND
BIDEN

THE STRUGGLE
CONTINUES

B*eyond Biden* was written in the spirit of Prime Minister Winston Churchill, who told students at Harrow School, his alma mater, on October 29, 1941, "Never give in. Never give in. Never, never, never, never—in nothing, great or small, large or petty—never give in, except to convictions of honour and good sense. Never yield to force. Never yield to the apparently overwhelming might of the enemy."[1]

Churchill articulated better than I could my reaction to the outrageous, one-sided, establishment takeover of the 2020 election.

Standing with my wife, Callista, in the White House on election night, we decided that we must look forward. We must learn the lessons of the immediate past, develop new and better strategies, and work with the American people to create a better future. We had to do this despite the temporary damage that would be caused by the radical left in all its forms: the oligarchs of internet censorship and propaganda, the false news media, crazed

Hollywood entertainers, ultra-woke college professors, the corrupt teachers' unions, and the left-wing bureaucrats who suffered four years under President Donald Trump and now had a chance to reimpose their collective will on Americans.

After observing the first year of Joe Biden's presidency, I am convinced the 2020 election was a detour, and not a turning point.

America has been through many cycles of challenge and response. No matter how long the odds, no matter how intense the opposition, Americans have always found a way to fight back, to become more creative, to respond to challenges, and to win.

So, I decided to focus my energy and attention on the time beyond Biden. If we do our jobs, that time could be an era in which the radical left will have destroyed itself, and a new, positive, problem-solving, and opportunity-creating system supported by an American majority could create several generations of prosperity, safety, and American revival.

As I thought and observed more, I felt compelled to write *Beyond Biden*.

Too many of my conservative friends were depressed and in despair about America's future. Seeing Biden leave his basement and be sworn in as president of the United States had emboldened every deranged left-wing radical to come from hiding and begin demanding that the government impose profoundly destructive values and ideas on Americans.

Many Republicans and conservatives were too tied up in the presidential election to notice that Kevin McCarthy's leadership in the U.S. House of Representatives—combined with unusually strong turnout for President Trump in key districts—had led to a gain of fifteen seats. Before the election, virtually every supposed expert thought Republicans would lose more than a dozen seats.

This left Speaker Nancy Pelosi with the narrowest majority since the 106th Congress in 2000. In the U.S. Senate, we fought to a tie. If it had not been for confused, self-defeating, and poorly run efforts by Republicans in Georgia, we would have had a 52 to 48 majority in the Senate.

When it came to controlling governorships, we had gained one and held a 27 to 23 majority across the nation. Republican-led states were doing far better economically and in health outcomes than the Democrat-run states were. Furthermore, Republican legislatures and governors were pushing back on radical, unpopular programs—and making their states more conservative despite Biden's and the national Democrats' best efforts.

Among state legislatures, there were 4,009 Republican legislators after the 2020 elections vs. 3,317 Democrats. In fact, Republican control of legislative chambers went up to 61 majorities compared with 37 Democrat chambers (Alaska has a unique multiparty sharing system, so it is not counted). With Republicans representing 54.3 percent of all state legislators and Democrats representing only 44.93 percent, it is hard to see why the left-wing media thinks Republicans have electoral problems.[2]

Republicans can look to the future confident that their party has a much broader appeal in the country at large. The left's power and influence is restricted to Washington, D.C., New York, and Los Angeles, where media centers prop up their morale with misleading and slanted reporting and analysis.

Further, as radical activists grow bolder and more open, their positions become more unpopular. We are already seeing a rejection of Critical Race Theory as more people realize it is primarily divisive. The mayor of Chicago refusing to be interviewed by white reporters is so blatantly racist it is starting to reshape the entire national debate about the importance of skin color.[3] President Biden's decision to cancel the Keystone XL pipeline while approving a Russian pipeline reminds people of the gap between Trump's America-first policy and what seems to be Biden's America-last policy. Increasing inflation is already worrying the American people. The gasoline shortages caused by the hacking of the Colonial Pipeline in Georgia brought an immediate reminder of President Jimmy Carter and his failures. The list goes on.

The ideological prejudice of the national Democrats, coupled with their belief in a world that doesn't exist, will likely lead to a pragmatic performance failure of historic scale. Consider the left's rejection of every policing reform Mayor Rudy Giuliani and Police Chief Bill Bratton used in dramatically turning around crime in New York City in the nineties. The left wants to cut the police, impose greater legal risks on being a policeman, disparage the police publicly, support district attorneys who refuse to prosecute crimes, and establish no-bail systems where criminals are put back on the street as soon as they arrive at the police station. Then they are shocked that an anti-police, pro-criminal policy leads to historic rates of increased crime.

Consider the impact of teachers' unions who fought going back to school for a year, regularly protect the most mediocre and incompetent teachers, try to impose radical values on students (even those in kindergarten and first grade), and dumb down courses when they fail to teach them. The result is too many students fail to learn and are weakened for life in terms of getting a job, being an informed citizen, and having a fair chance to rise.

For these reasons alone, I am certain there will soon be a beyond Biden period.

IS THIS BOOK FOR YOU?

All too often we are told America is divided into red vs. blue.

I am a conservative, and I have cheerfully spent my entire career as a partisan. However, this book is written to convince you that America is much bigger than the red-blue, Republican-Democrat, conservative-liberal dichotomy. There is an American majority, a red, white, and blue unity, which the news media and politicians refuse to work with—and perhaps are too ideologically blind to see.

Here is a small test that will help you decide whether you could be part of the American majority. See if you agree or disagree with the following ten statements.

1. Americans should be judged by Rev. Martin Luther King Jr.'s standard: the content of their character, not the color of their skin.
2. Needy but able-bodied adults should still have to work to receive taxpayer-funded benefits such as food stamps, free health care, or welfare.
3. America is the greatest country on earth.
4. Criminals who kill police officers should have mandatory life imprisonment.
5. Federal income taxes should be cut for all Americans.
6. There should be tax credits for products manufactured in America.
7. Valid government-issued photo identification should be required to vote in elections.
8. People should be able to freely practice their religion.
9. All children should have the opportunity to go to the schools that are best for them.

10. Noncitizen gang members, such as members of
    MS-13, should face mandatory deportation when
    they are arrested.

If you agreed with at least seven of these statements, this book is for you. If you agreed with four or more, you may find this book intriguing. You may find an amazingly different take on America than you will ever see portrayed in the elite national media.

Otherwise, you may not want to read this book—although I encourage you to do so. You may simply reject the idea that you could be this far from the thinking of the majority of Americans. But, I'm afraid you are.

In early 2021, Gingrich 360 started working with McLaughlin & Associates on an important project. We asked them to survey people nationwide to find super-majority issues that bring together the American majority—across all ages, ethnicities, and political affiliations. Naturally, we are calling it the American Majority Project. Consider how the American majority answered the previous questions.

- 91 percent of Americans believe Rev. King was right about the content of your character being more important than the color of your skin.
- 74 percent believe able-bodied adults should be required to work for government benefits.
- 78 percent say America is the greatest country on earth.
- 74 percent favor mandatory life sentences for cop killers.
- 75 percent of Americans favor federal income tax cuts.
- 87 percent want tax credits for products made in America.

- 81 percent of Americans say photo identification should be required for voting.
- 85 percent say government should protect religious freedom.
- 81 percent of Americans want children to have the choice to go to schools that are right for them.
- 87 percent favor mandatory deportation for noncitizen gang members.

On these ten questions (and we have many more that fit this pattern) the American majority ranges from 74.3 percent to 91.2 percent of Americans. The average for these ten is above 80 percent. Without the constant, intense, and sometimes ferocious efforts of the left, a people-oriented American system would clearly be far more patriotic and far more conservative than anything the Washington elites can imagine.

An American government that followed the wishes of the American people would have dramatically different policies (in many cases, completely opposite policies) from the current power structure, which is hostile to the common culture and beliefs of most Americans.

Beyond Biden is an effort to describe the kind of America that is possible if we embrace the values and system favored by the majority of the American people.

This is a process that is already under way in a number of states governed by conservatives, who are reasserting American values and American goals. *Beyond Biden* also outlines the challenges we face and the values and policies the American people will support in meeting those challenges.

PART I

WE WILL WIN AGAIN

CHAPTER ONE

YOU AIN'T SEEN NOTHING YET

All too many conservatives have reacted to the rise of radicalism within the Democratic Party with a sense of despair. They behave as though losing the presidential battle of 2020 was the end of the great American journey.

This simply isn't so. We have been here before, and we have rebounded. We will win again.

I am confident we will win because the Joe Biden–Kamala Harris–Chuck Schumer–Nancy Pelosi system has three major fatal flaws:

1. It is permeated with a sense of dishonesty about the nature of America and its people.
2. It naturally creates so-called solutions that make problems worse.
3. Because of the first two problems, it has an inability to deal with the real world and get important things done.

As a young candidate in the 1970s, I watched the American left implode because of these same three characteristics. The aftermath of the Vietnam War and Watergate combined with the first Arab oil embargo had broken the Republican momentum coming out of the massive victory in 1972 over George McGovern.

I was a candidate for Congress in 1974 and lost during Watergate (with 48.5 percent of the vote against the dean of the Georgia delegation, a Democrat). I was a candidate for Congress again in 1976 with Georgia governor Jimmy Carter at the head of the Democratic ticket sweeping Georgia. I lost again (with 48.2 percent of the vote).

In what may have been the last campaign of my thus far unsuccessful political career, I ran again in 1978. The dean of the delegation who previously beat me retired, and the Democrats nominated a liberal state senator. President Carter had proven to be too liberal for Americans. With gasoline lines, energy prices skyrocketing, and other problems beginning to build, I finally won (with 54 percent of the vote).

The U.S. House Republican Party I joined in December 1978 was shattered by Watergate and Vietnam, split by the Gerald Ford–Ronald Reagan presidential nomination fight in 1976, and demoralized by the number of Republican colleagues who had retired or been defeated. Things were not looking good.

At the depths of Republican despair along came Reagan and the world changed. It is vital to remember President Reagan's belief in the spirit of the American people. On November 5, 1984, the eve of the election, President Reagan addressed the country, saying:

"Our opponents have a very different vision for your future. Where we look at a problem and see opportunity, they look at opportunity and see a problem. We believe in knowing when opportunity knocks. They seem determined to knock opportunity. . . . We can say to the world and pledge to our children, America's best days lie ahead, and you ain't seen nothing yet." [1]

It is easy to forget what an amazing change that was from a mere four years earlier. In the constant political din, it's also easy to forget how the next six years would validate President Reagan's optimism.

Contrast the positive view of Reagan with President Carter's so-called "malaise speech." On July 15, 1979, President Carter addressed the nation during a growing economic crisis. There was a profound sense in the country that things were starting to fall apart. In a tone exactly the opposite of Reagan's cheerful optimism, Carter warned:

"The threat is nearly invisible in ordinary ways. It is a crisis of confidence. It is a crisis that strikes at the very heart and soul and spirit of our national will. We can see this crisis in the growing doubt about the meaning of our own lives and in the loss of a unity of purpose for our nation. The erosion of our confidence in the future is threatening to destroy the social and the political fabric of America." [2]

Carter described that "the symptoms of this crisis of the American spirit are all around us." And he gravely said, "There are no short-term solutions to our long-range problems. There is simply no way to avoid sacrifice."

So, in the contest between Reagan's optimistic vision of a better future and Carter's promise of everyone having to sacrifice, Reagan had an enormous advantage. He was offering "more and better" while President Carter was offering a smaller future with government-controlled rationing, higher taxes, and pain.

As candidate Reagan put it in 1980: "Recession is when your neighbor loses his job. Depression is when you lose yours. And recovery is when Jimmy Carter loses his."[3] America agreed with Reagan, who won in the largest electoral college landslide against an incumbent president (489-49). This helped gain 12 U.S. Senate seats, making Senator Howard Baker the majority leader, and Republicans gained 35 House seats. Reagan's principles and policies were so effective that by 1984 he was running on "Morning in America" as his theme.

It is hard to remember now, but Reagan supported Federal Reserve chairman Paul Volcker in defeating inflation through a deeply painful recession caused by high interest rates. He then launched what turned into a twenty-five-year economic boom by cutting taxes and regulations to encourage investment, productivity, and job creation.

In foreign policy the difference was even more striking. President Carter was confronted by an expansionist Soviet Union from Afghanistan, to Angola, to Central America, and even into Western Europe politically. The Soviets believed the correlation of forces was moving to their advantage. The newly made Iranian religious dictatorship seized the American embassy and held American diplomats hostage while Carter seemed weak and ineffective. The hostages were released the day Reagan was inaugurated. Within eleven years, the Soviet Union literally disappeared on December 25, 1991.[4]

There is every reason to believe the Carter-Reagan cycle will be repeated as the radicalism of the Democrats, the pain of their economic policies, and the costs of their weakness in national security and foreign policy all create deep dissatisfaction among the American people.

The lesson from the extraordinary rise of Reagan, the success of his positive vision of America's future, and the impact of sound conservative principles is simple: A positive, optimistic, problem-solving, and life-improving conservatism can attract a huge majority that rejects the pain and anti-American hostility of the militant left—and which attracts support through a vision of a better future.

It is possible to create a "better future" conservative movement, because the underlying patterns of progress are so powerful despite every effort of the American left to use government to create a smaller, poorer, bureaucrat-controlled left-wing America.

THE BETTER FUTURE OPPORTUNITIES

We really "ain't seen nothing yet." We are on the edge of a series of scientific and technological revolutions that will make our lives dramatically more enjoyable. The potential from science and technology will be reinforced by the dramatic improvements that occur as we leave the left-wing policies that fail and return to the conservative policies that succeed. Consider just some of the areas in which the future could suddenly become much better.

The development of artificial intelligence, quantum computing, augmented reality, and robotics will synergistically reinforce themselves and create waves of new opportunities and services. Think back to the worldwide development of automatic teller machines, the rise of personal computing with video capabilities, the emergence of distance health, distance surgery, and the emergence of enhanced driving capabilities in cars. Each of these enhanced our capabilities and our choices. The wave of change is accelerating not shrinking. More rapid breakthroughs are going to make bureaucratic rigidity and paperwork more destructive. New science and technology require an entrepreneurial spirit to be driven into society and government. The miracle of the COVID-19 vaccine discovery, manufacture, and distribution is a good case study.

President Trump's entrepreneurial drive for the earliest possible vaccine against COVID-19 led to amazing results. He had been told it would take three to five years following the normal bureaucratic rules. When he said we would have a vaccine in one year, the bureaucratic, media, establishment world scoffed and called him a liar. He got it done in less than a year by three parallel efforts producing three different vaccines. He forced the Food and Drug Administration to break out of its bureaucratic patterns. The Trump entrepreneurial attitude cut the traditional red tape and revealed the "three to five years" bureaucratic system as inhumane, uncompassionate, and completely unacceptable. As an entrepreneur himself, President Trump understood that the federal government guaranteeing payment allowed the drug companies to make massive investments at minimum risk. He knew this would guarantee mass production of the vaccines. The Trump gamble paid off in saving hundreds of thousands of lives around the world.

There are other areas in which we have successful models of achieving dramatic improvements. For various reasons, many of these successes are unacceptable to the left because they challenge left-wing ideology or interest groups. For example, the left is ideologically committed to a series of anti-police, pro-criminal domestic policies (eliminating bail, defunding police, decriminalizing theft and drug use, and others). The primary problem is these policies directly lead to steady increases in crime and reductions in public safety. The American left's interest groups such as Black Lives Matter, anti-law district attorneys, the American Civil Liberties Union, and others are passionately opposed to policies that work to reduce crime.

With rational, conservative, pro-law, anti-crime policies, crime will diminish dramatically, and public safety can improve almost overnight. We know that when Mayor Rudy Giuliani and Chief Bill Bratton set out to dramatically reduce crime in New York they applied a set of principles that reduced murders by 85 percent over time. We know that these principles work whenever they have been applied. We also know that the left's policies will radically increase the crime rate. In fact, we see it already happening. It is time to move once again to policies that keep the public safe.

The new focus on fighting crime should extend to white-collar crime. Consider that during the COVID-19 crisis, criminals stole as much as half of the unemployment dollars released by the federal government. As Felix Salmon reported for Axios, "Unemployment fraud during the pandemic could easily reach $400 billion, according to some estimates, and the bulk of the money likely ended [up] in the hands of foreign crime syndicates—making this not just theft, but a matter of national security."[5]

The shock of this will eventually lead America to a deep reassertion that honesty matters, and that systems of theft and corruption should be relentlessly tracked down and punished.

On a more positive front, breakthroughs in science and organization will improve health to an almost unbelievable degree. The science and study of aging is rapidly maturing and will presently extend human life by a decade or more. Maybe even more important, if we can postpone aging for a decade, we postpone diabetes, Parkinson's, many cancers, and other maladies that we now understand are a result of aging. We will see health span improve even more dramatically than life span.

Further, the study of the brain is rapidly reaching a point where we can anticipate a substantial decline in Alzheimer's, Parkinson's, and other brain-related diseases. Since many other physical diseases are a function of our mental health, the improvement in knowledge of the brain will enable us to have remarkably healthier, more independent lives.

Just as scientific breakthroughs have made heart disease, contagious diseases, many cancers, and other manifestations of bad health more manageable, curable, and/or preventable, we are going to see the complete eradication or control of a number of illnesses.

As our ability to manage health improves, so will our ability to control costs. When transparency of costs and quality enable individuals to seek the best treatment at the lowest cost, the natural pattern of a competitive market will drive down prices (LASIK surgery is a great example of how competition and transparency have lowered prices).

The return to an energy policy that encourages the production of American energy will have both an economic and a national security advantage. You will pay less at the pump, have better jobs, and America will be safer from foreign blackmail. This was at the heart of my book *Drill Here, Drill Now, Pay Less* in 2008. It is still true today.

Rejecting race-based politics and policies will return America to an integrated future in which every American has an opportunity to pursue happiness. Despite all the noise in the media, among professional race-focused politicians, and other members of the racism industry, the vast majority of Americans seek a post-racial future. (Remember: By 91 percent to 5 percent, Americans agree with Rev. Martin Luther King Jr.'s dream that his children "will one day live in a nation where they will not be judged by the color of their skin but by the content of their character.")

As the new racists sharpen the choice and the cost of tolerating left-wing racism becomes clear, Americans will consolidate around the desire for a successful American society rather than a collection of racially defined tribes. The impact of this consolidation of values will be amazing.

Schools will return to focusing on merit, earned grades, and achievement rather than brainwashing children. The *New York Times*' 1619 Project will be abandoned as historically false and racist propaganda. The Trump administration's 1776 Commission (or something akin to it) will be reestablished, and teaching factually sound, patriotic American history will once again become the norm. The goal of President Trump's 1776 Commission was to inform Americans of what is universally true and good about the American experiment and placed the battle to end slavery and discrimination within that framework.

Critical Race Theory will be recognized as racist and destructive and will be outlawed in virtually every school district. Leftwing "woke" colleges and universities will come under enormous pressure to return to teaching classic American history and values. Boards of trustees and other leaders will put pressure on anti-American ideologues in higher education. Students will have greater rights to challenge efforts at brainwashing.

In the meantime, the collapse of effective education, and the greed and selfish interests of the teachers' unions, will lead to massive support for school choice in K–12 education followed by a dramatic improvement in learning outcomes. For higher learning, the combination of constant scientific and technological progress—and the failure of so many schools to educate adequately for the last two decades—will lead to a new expansion of in-person and virtual learning for adults to enable them to find good jobs in the rapidly evolving economy.

Efforts to establish race-based reparations will be deeply opposed as Americans focus on helping the poor regardless of background—and solving the weaknesses that lead to lower incomes and fewer opportunities to advance. As a result of a multifaceted effort to correct the disastrous policies of liberalism, life will become much better for people without money (the concept of "the poor" will gradually disappear as we learn once again that poverty and success is cultural and learned). Americans will focus on learning how to acquire money and learning how to build neighborhoods and communities that are functional and productive. South Carolina Republican senator Tim Scott's 10,000 opportunity zones project (when combined with lower taxes, less red tape, and dramatic improvements in safety) will create local jobs and much safer neighborhoods.

For those who need it, getting money from government will be tied to a work requirement (as we did with welfare reform in 1996). The goal of welfare programs will be to get people out of the system rather than into the system. There will be a steady effort to make work a core value, so people acquire the skills and habits of successfully working and earning their way to better and better jobs. Connecting work to getting government money will lead to radical reductions in homelessness and dependence on government. Since getting money from government will require earning the money, the perverse incentive to be unemployed and dependent will diminish rapidly.

The revolution in science and technology will lead to parallel revolutions in both national security and space. As a result, America will be safer, its ability to lead the planet will be strengthened, and the economic and tourist opportunities in space will explode with opportunities for the next generation to engage in a great adventure.

Within thirty years, Americans and their allies will routinely be manufacturing in space and colonizing the moon and Mars. The first steps will have been taken to mining asteroids. Space tourism will have become a significant business both in near-earth brief experiences and in traveling to a space station or to the moon or Mars. The space industry by 2050 will be a multi-trillion-dollar business.

I hope this swift tour of the possibilities for dramatic, positive change whets your appetite for a resurgent, confident American future that will meet President Reagan's challenge, "We can say to the world and pledge to our children, America's best days lie ahead, and you ain't seen nothing yet."

CHAPTER TWO

BIPARTISAN BALONEY

T his is meant to be a positive, optimistic book. But to describe what we can fix—and how we can achieve the prosperous, people-focused country that we want—we must discuss what is broken and identify what is keeping us from uniting.

When President Joe Biden was inaugurated, I was asked what I thought of his speech and what we should expect from his administration and leadership. Biden had campaigned for months—and just given a strong inaugural speech—on leading as a bipartisan president who would represent the interests of all Americans.

His inaugural left me with the same impression I had of President Barack Obama's first inaugural address. As a historian and a practitioner of politics, I commented at the time that if Obama actually led the way he said he would (as a moderate pragmatist, guided by bipartisanship and civility), he would split Republicans in Washington and build an enormous, popular governing coalition that would keep power for decades. Similarly, I said if Biden led as America's president rather than the Democratic Party's president, he would get a tremendous amount done and reorder Washington in a way his predecessor failed to do.

As I'm writing this, nearly seven months into President Biden's first year in office, it is clear he has no intention of doing what he said he would.

In his inaugural address, Biden said:

"Today, on this January day, my whole soul is in this: Bringing America together. Uniting our people. And uniting our nation. I ask every American to join me in this cause. Uniting to fight the common foes we face: Anger, resentment, hatred. Extremism, lawlessness, violence. Disease, joblessness, hopelessness. With unity we can do great things. Important things. We can right wrongs. We can put people to work in good jobs. We can teach our children in safe schools. We can overcome this deadly virus. We can reward work, rebuild the middle class, and make health care secure for all. We can deliver racial justice. We can make America, once again, the leading force for good in the world."[1]

However, since his first day in office, he has done nothing to unify our nation. He has instead aggressively pushed an agenda that appeals only to the Democratic Party's most radical members. On the same day that he pledged to unite us, Biden signed seventeen executive actions. A few of them were rational actions to combat the COVID-19 pandemic or relieve Americans struggling because of it. These include his 100-day masking challenge, and his extension of the Trump administration's halts on evictions, foreclosures, and student loan debt payments and interest. (A federal court later ruled the halt on evictions was an overreach by the Centers for Disease Control and Prevention.)

However, most of Biden's first-day executive actions were purely partisan Democrat agenda items—and nine were direct reversals of broadly supported actions that the previous administration had put in place around immigration, travel during the pandemic, and regulatory reforms.

On day one, Biden said the United States would rejoin the Paris Climate Accord, which his former boss had first joined and President Trump left. U.S. involvement in the Paris agreement has been hotly debated since its inception. Many Americans—including independents and Democrats—believe the United States should not enter treaty-like agreements while skirting the constitutional rules for entering treaties (which require approval of the U.S. Senate). Others specifically had concerns that joining the Paris agreement would force America to accept stringent and costly environmental standards, while other countries that were bigger polluters would get a pass. As for rejoining the Paris agreement specifically, only 55 percent of Americans said they would support rejoining the accord in a November 2020 YouGov Poll. Of that number, 79 percent were Democrats and only 21 percent were Republicans.[2] There was nothing bipartisan about this decision.

Following the Paris decision, President Biden then canceled all permits for the Keystone XL Pipeline. In a reverse image of the Paris decision, Obama had first canceled this project, and President Trump reinstated it. The pipeline would have carried crude oil from Alberta, Canada, to another pipeline in Nebraska, and ultimately to the coasts of Texas and Louisiana to be refined.

This would have continued to make the United States less dependent on dangerous oil-rich nations abroad (led by people who hate us). The pipeline would have also made transporting oil from our northern neighbor to refineries in the Gulf easier, safer, and cleaner. Moving oil by pipeline allows you to avoid putting it aboard large ships, tanker trucks, or trains, which can crash with disastrous results to the environment, communities, and human life. Just imagine if the ship that grounded in the Suez Canal earlier this year had been a tanker filled with crude oil. It would have created a far more serious, prolonged crisis.

As the BBC reported after Biden's decision to cancel the project's permits, the pipeline would have also reduced the price of oil—and some estimated it would have potentially created nearly 30,000 construction jobs in the American Midwest.[3] On the first day of Biden's presidency, a barrel of oil cost $55.22. As I'm writing this in July 2021, the price is $74.93, a nearly 36 percent increase. There is currently no indication that a price ceiling is in sight.

Setting aside the merits of the pipeline project, Biden's action was in no way bipartisan. In 2017, the last time a major survey addressed the pipeline, Americans were split on the subject. According to Pew Research, 42 percent of Americans favored building the pipeline, while 48 percent opposed it. Importantly, support for the pipeline had dropped because the project had become a divisive political symbol during the Obama administration. According to Pew:

"Support for Keystone XL has fallen since 2014, largely because of a sharp decline among Democrats and Democratic-leaning independents. The share of the overall public favoring the pipeline has fallen 17 percentage points since 2014 (from 59% to 42%). Just 17% of Democrats favor building the pipeline, less than half the share that did so three years ago (44%)."[4]

In this case, Biden was doing what his Democratic base wanted and ignoring the rest of us. This decision may come back to haunt him. After all, he killed a lucrative, wealth- and job-creating project during a pandemic and a shutdown-driven economic depression. In April 2021, Gallup reported that Americans are split on whether the strength of the economy or the health of the environment should get priority (42 percent are for jobs, while 50 percent favor environmental protection). Further, Gallup said willingness to place the environment over jobs was being driven down sharply by the strain of prolonged high unemployment and economic decline.

"Both party groups are more likely than they were a year ago to prioritize the economy. However, the current percentages are starkly different: 68% of Republicans (up from 54% a year ago) vs. 23% of Democrats (up from 16%) now say the economy should have precedence. Meanwhile, 22% of Republicans (down from 36% in 2020) vs. 71% of Democrats (down from 81%) prioritize the environment," according to Gallup's Lydia Saad.[5]

This decision was also not lost on some of the largest American unions (who had supported Biden in the election). The North American Building Trades Unions, the Laborers' International Union of North America, and the United Association of Union Plumbers and Pipefitters all denounced Biden's decision to kill the pipeline project.

UAUPP general president Mark McManus said:

"In revoking this permit, the Biden Administration has chosen to listen to the voices of fringe activists instead of union members and the American consumer on Day 1. Let me be very clear: When built with union labor by the men and women of the United Association, pipelines like Keystone XL remain the safest and most efficient modes of energy transportation in the world. Sadly, the Biden Administration has now put thousands of union workers out of work. For the average American family, it means energy costs will go up and communities will no longer see the local investments that come with pipeline construction."[6]

This was not the action of a president working to create American jobs or improve the lives of Americans. It was the action of a president seeking to appease an increasingly radical base.

President Biden, also on day one, recommitted the United States to funding the World Health Organization. From 2018 to 2019, the United States provided $893 million to the organization, accounting for 20 percent of its total budget. For perspective, the United Kingdom, Germany, and Japan combined provided roughly 22 percent of the WHO's budget. Biden's decision to renew funding for WHO was deeply divisive given the WHO's willingness to peddle Chinese Communist Party propaganda about the initial spread of COVID-19. While the organization has become more vigilant about China's propaganda efforts regarding the virus, at the time Biden decided to rejoin, WHO was still providing cover for the Chinese Communist Party's lies about the virus.

As Zachary Faria wrote for the *Washington Examiner* on January 14, 2021:

"One year ago today, the World Health Organization lied to the world about the coronavirus. Some 2 million deaths later, the organization still hasn't learned much from its failures.

"On Jan. 14, 2020, the WHO uncritically parroted Chinese propaganda as the world watched China's coronavirus outbreak with some concern. In the tweet, which still has not been deleted, the WHO says that 'Chinese authorities have found no clear evidence of human-to-human transmission' of the coronavirus.

"Doctors in Wuhan, China, had evidence of human-to-human transmission of the virus as early as the first week of December 2019. The WHO still praised China's response to the virus as its leaders privately complained about the Chinese Communist Party's lack of transparency. China blocked outside health experts and covered up the spread of the virus, all while declaring that other countries brought the virus to China."[7]

Further, this was not a unifying move for Americans. In June 2020, when the United States broke ties with the global health bureaucracy, Pew Research reported that only 46 percent of Americans gave the WHO good marks for its handling of the COVID-19 crisis. A full 70 percent of right-leaning Americans who were polled disapproved of WHO's performance while 36 percent of Democrats were unhappy with the organization.[8]

The most divisive of his day one actions concerned immigration and border security. In a flurry of executive actions, Biden decreed that noncitizens must be counted in the U.S. Census, dashing the Trump administration's effort to keep people in the country illegally from being counted for congressional apportionment. Biden halted construction of the wall at the U.S.-Mexico border, and pulled back immigration enforcement activities.

First, immigration and border security have been starkly partisan issues for decades—although they have become more polarizing in recent years. In fact, Populace's 2021 American Aspirations Index found that immigration was the single most polarizing topic in American politics today. The Massachusetts-based think tank found that across a series of immigration-related topics, the left and right were fully at odds. The survey asked 2,010 Americans to rank 55 of America's priorities from most important (1) to least important (55). When asked if the United States should be open to immigration, Biden voters ranked it 27th most important, while Trump voters ranked it 52nd most important. Having secure national borders was the No. 2 most important priority for Trump voters, while it was 31st for Biden supporters. "Severely restricting immigration" was the third highest priority for Trump voters, while it was ranked 46th for Biden voters.[9]

As Axios reported about the Populace survey, "Americans have surprisingly similar priorities for the U.S., but immigration stands out as one of the few issues with clear partisan differences. It underscores the challenge for advocates and lawmakers hoping to pass immigration reform in the coming weeks amid narrow margins in Congress."[10]

Biden's early actions on immigration remain among his most unpopular. In February 2021, Morning Consult found that only

45 percent of Americans supported including undocumented immigrants in the U.S. Census. Forty-two percent opposed this action and 13 percent weren't sure. Only 51 percent supported ending construction on the border wall, while 38 percent opposed, and 11 percent had no opinion. Similar splits existed with Biden's decisions to:

- end the "remain in Mexico policy" (46 percent support, 41 percent oppose);
- review the "public charge rule," which ensures that immigrants entering the county do not become dependent on the state (49 percent support, 35 percent oppose);
- and end the travel ban to some Muslim-majority countries (48 percent support, 39 percent oppose).

While it didn't happen on day one, Morning Consult found the least popular action Biden had taken by February was his decision to expand the cap on the number of refugees America would accept in the coming year from 15,000 to 125,000. Only 39 percent of Americans supported this decision while 48 percent rejected it.[11] Five of his seven least popular executive actions involved changes to immigration policy from the Trump era.

No one who is serious about bringing the country together, bridging divides, and finding common ground would take such aggressive actions on the most divisive aspect of American domestic policy on his first day in office.

President Biden could have taken a lesson from Republicans when we drafted the Contract with America in 1994. When we were building the Contract, we refused to include any issue that didn't have 70 percent or better support from the American people. I believe this decision was crucial to the Republicans' success in 1994, when we took back the U.S. House majority for the first time in forty years. We are following a similar model now for the American Majority Project leading into the 2022 and 2024 elections.

As a final example, President Biden rescinded the 1776 Commission report. Unfortunately, the basic facts of American history have become partisan battlegrounds. For decades now, radical elites in academia (and now media) have been working to rewrite America's history so that our Founding Fathers become villains, our founding documents become tools of oppression, and our basic freedoms become perverse privileges that only benefit those in power. It has been a protracted act of cultural warfare designed to give radical elites license to revise our history and reorder our country into a place guided by ideology rather than reality—and a place that serves ideologues rather than We the People.

The 1776 Commission was convened specifically to rebut these efforts—notably the *New York Times'* 1619 Project, which numerous historians have denounced as deeply flawed. (In fact, some of the falsehoods in the project's collection of essays were so indefensible the *New York Times* has quietly edited the most egregious untruths online.)[12] In its original form, the project claimed that the "true founding" of America was when the first British ship carrying slaves docked in New England in 1619. It also argued that the American Revolution was fought in defense of slavery—rather than over Americans' right to rule themselves with a government elected by, for, and of the People. The project also made the ridiculous argument that the slave trade served as the foundation of American capitalism (a claim that anyone familiar with history would recognize as complete nonsense).

There are many legitimate academic arguments about the particular origins of modern capitalism—whether it came from Dutch merchants who developed a novel commercial trading system, mercantilism, and other trade systems used during the Renaissance, or later out of Adam Smith's *An Inquiry into the Nature and Causes of the Wealth of Nations* and other works. These are all interesting arguments worthy of debate. However, if you boil capitalism down to the basic idea that individuals can own property and wealth, use that wealth to create goods and services, and trade those goods and services to enrich themselves, then capitalism has existed for about as long as human history. In fact, the ancient Chinese could be considered some of the earliest capitalists. The society and culture of the Roman Empire was largely driven by individuals who bought property and amassed wealth to trade. So, the notion that American capitalism is somehow uniquely rooted to the colonial slave trade is so full of ignorance, it is almost not worth arguing against—but for the danger of allowing ignorance to propagate.

The 1776 Commission was an effort by a group of eighteen patriotic and respected American academics, journalists, and policy experts who sought to protect and promote an unbiased, accurate curriculum for American history. It by no means sought to erase the institution of slavery from our history—or any other ugly or reprehensible part of America's story. But it did reinforce the centuries-old, widely accepted views that our Founding Fathers worked to create a new nation in which free people could shape their own destinies through hard work—and that our inalienable human rights were given by our Creator, not a monarch or government.

The 1776 Commission sought to support the notion that America is an imperfect nation, which is constantly working toward perfection. Our Founders were far from perfect. They were human beings with merits and flaws living in an era far different and more hostile than our own. But they still created a nation unlike any other in their time, which was built around individual liberty and the notion that people could govern themselves. The Declaration of Independence and the U.S. Constitution shook the foundations of society around the world—and have helped export liberty and democracy for 245 years.

As you can imagine, the idea that we should revise our history to agree with a modern political narrative is not a unifying one. As the *Daily Signal* reported, a Heritage Foundation survey found most parents and school board members reject the idea that the 1619 Project should be included in school curriculum.

> "The survey, conducted of 1,001 parents and 566 school board members, revealed that much of the nation is divided in its opinions of the 1619 Project.
>
> "When asked whether 1776 should continue to be taught as the year of the country's founding, rather than 1619, 59.1% of parents and 72.6% of school board members answered the year the Declaration of Independence was signed should remain as America's founding date.
>
> "Almost 50% of parents and 70% of school board members said they do not want their children's school to use instructional material based on the idea that slavery is the 'center of our national narrative.'"[13]

Unfortunately, Biden's partisan agenda only continued. By his one hundredth day in office, President Biden had taken 65 executive actions—24 of which were direct reversals of Trump administration policies.[14] Specifically, he signed 52 executive orders or memorandums. For comparison, this is 13 more than President Trump, 18 more than Obama, and 39 more than President George W. Bush had signed in their first hundred days.

THE PHONY LANDSLIDE

Part of the reason President Biden immediately tossed out the idea of unifying the country is that the Democrats, the media, Big Tech, and academia have all been operating in a false reality in which the 2020 election was a landslide victory for the American left.

On November 4, 2020, the left declared victory over President Trump and began an aggressive march to undo virtually every positive conservative achievement from the previous four years—and impose a future for America that most Americans simply do not want. They have treated President Biden's win as though it were a mandate from the American people to aggressively pursue a radical agenda. But 2020 wasn't a landslide—certainly not for the left.

More than 74 million people voted for President Trump. In addition, Republicans made important gains in the House that suggest most Americans do not want the Biden–Kamala Harris–Nancy Pelosi–Chuck Schumer vision for America—they simply were unhappy with Trump. This is something the left and its allies in the media have simply not been able to accept or acknowledge.

Prior to the 2020 election, no presidential candidate had ever received more than 69 million votes (President Barack Obama's record set in 2008). Yet Trump earned 74 million in 2020—the most of any incumbent president in history. President Biden's supporters will quickly note he earned 81 million—or 7 million more than Trump.

Naturally, with unprecedented numbers of people voting by mail; a house-bound and frustrated populace; and a deeply aggressive political media hell-bent on enraging every single American for ratings, big numbers should have been expected. For the first time in more than one hundred years, voter turnout reached nearly 66 percent. More Americans voted than in any election in our nation's history. To be clear: large voter turnout is good. In every election, every single person who can legally vote should be able to easily and securely. However, states across the nation were simply not prepared to handle this election in a way that conveyed confidence to voters that the elections were secure and accurate.

So, from myriad angles, the 2020 presidential election was profoundly historic. Yet, the news and social media, academia, and establishment institutions uniformly focused on one aspect— the only one they cared about—that Trump lost. The story was clear from the start: The 51 percent of Americans who voted for Biden matter. The 49 percent who didn't vote for Biden do not matter—and on the left it was decreed that those who specifically voted for Trump are a threat to democracy.

The January 6, 2021, attack on the U.S. Capitol building only reinforced this dynamic. The few hundred misguided protestors who became lawbreakers who stormed the U.S. Capitol could now be used by the left as shorthand to represent any of the 74 million who voted for Trump. The establishment cultural powers embraced this narrative, because it was the natural continuation of the mantra they had already been reciting for nearly five years.

ASSERTING THE AMERICAN MAJORITY

In early May, the Biden administration did two things that clarified something alarming for me. First, the administration canceled an agreement between South Dakota and the U.S. National Park Service to host a fireworks show to be held at Mount Rushmore on the Fourth of July. I spoke with Governor Kristi Noem, who told me that the administration had decided not to uphold the agreement, which had been reached under the previous administration.

I puzzled over this decision for a few days to try to understand why an American president would deny a request to have a safe, outdoor fireworks celebration at the national site. What is more patriotic than an image of fireworks exploding over the sculptures of four of our greatest presidents? Then it struck me: the event was canceled *because it was patriotic.* It's not so much that the Biden administration is anti-American. The Biden administration is anti-Americans—as in you and me. President Trump had called for the fireworks show at Mount Rushmore last year, for the first time in a decade. The only reason I could fathom that the members of the Biden administration didn't want to do it is because the half of America that they hate would go and enjoy it.

The other confounding decision the administration made was to in effect cancel the annual Rolling Thunder motorcycle parade in Washington, D.C., which was renamed this year to

"Rolling to Remember 2021." This is a Memorial Day motorcycle parade that has run for three decades to support America's veterans and raise awareness to the challenges they face. Again, this is one of the most patriotic public displays that exists in our modern culture.

The event was canceled in 2020 at the height of the COVID-19 pandemic and the Biden Pentagon cited the pandemic again in 2021 as a reason for denying participants access to its parking lot (which is one of the only spaces in the area that is large enough to accommodate the parade vehicles). However, AMVETS, the organization that now runs the event, reached out multiple times to demonstrate how it would use the space safely. The veterans' group had apparently put in the request to use the parking lot in July 2020. After getting no response from the Pentagon, the group finally heard back in April—just a month before the event. Jan Brown, the national commander of AMVETS, said, "The biggest disappointment in the Pentagon's denial was that AMVETS was ignored for months as its professional staff in Washington requested numerous times an opportunity to hear the Defense Department's concerns and present a [coronavirus] safety plan."[15]

In my many decades in American politics, I never could have imagined an administration that would deny a veterans group the right to put on this annual parade. But the American left has become unlike any prior American political movement. It is led by a militant minority and guided by a largely anti-American culture. It is well organized and good at using all the instruments of power it can to impose its anti-American ideology on the rest of us.

This explains Biden's immediate shift from unity to partisanship. It explains the cohesion among the media, academia, and Big Tech to promote the Democrats' agenda and silence dissent. And it explains the rising trend of anti-patriotism coming from the early days of the Biden administration—which is admittedly being driven by the administration and not the president himself.

However, there is a silver lining. The 2020 elections were largely failures for Democrats. After the elections, Republicans controlled both houses in 31 state legislatures and Minnesota, which is a split legislature. In 23 of those states, Republicans also control the governorship. For months leading up to November, virtually every elite political analyst was predicting that Pelosi's majority in the U.S. House of Representatives would grow by 15 seats. Instead, Republicans gained that amount. And many of those gains were made by women or Republican members of the Black and Hispanic communities.

As Henry Olsen wrote in *The Washington Post*:

"At least 33 House Republicans will be either women or non-White when the new body sits in January. This includes 27 women, six Hispanics, and two Black men, Burgess Owens of Utah and Byron Donalds of Florida. They come from all regions of the country and represent urban, suburban and rural seats.

"In fact, every seat Republicans have flipped from blue to red has been captured by a woman or a minority. This wasn't an accident. Aided by efforts by the National Republican Congressional Committee and Rep. Elise Stefanik (R-N.Y.), GOP officials strenuously tried to recruit capable female and non-White candidates for as many pickup opportunities as possible. These efforts could bear even more fruit, as two other women and one

Hispanic—Mariannette Miller-Meeks in Iowa, Claudia Tenney in New York and Mike Garcia in California— might still win the seats they are contesting."[16]

If you analyze the Democrats' actions in early 2021 you understand that they know their grasp on power is weak, and they are trying to force through everything they can before 2022. The scale of hostility is enormous, and the media (including social media) are silencing anyone who seems to be getting in the way. All indications point to Republican gains in the 2022 House elections, which could build momentum for a serious GOP win in 2024.

The truth is the country is already fairly unified on specific ideals. We are just being led by a radical minority. The American Majority is here—but it is being ignored. That's what *Beyond Biden* hopes to change.

CHAPTER THREE

THE MAD DASH
FOR POWER

President Biden's actions in his first hundred days in office were merely part of the effort to radically transform our nation. Congressional Democrats have been far more aggressive in gathering power and seeking to impose partisan ideology on the country. Speaker Pelosi and Senate Leader Schumer rarely, if ever, echoed President Biden's early claims of bipartisanship. There was never any illusion among congressional Democrats that unifying America was a goal. After all, these were the same politicians who spent much of the previous four years on partisan investigations, smear campaigns, and desperate attempts to unseat the duly elected forty-fifth president of the United States.

I also suspect Pelosi and Schumer had a clearer view of their futures. The Biden administration was celebrating a victory that would pay off for four years, but Pelosi and Schumer knew that the 2020 legislative elections did not go their way—and the 2022 elections would likely mean the end of Democrat control on Capitol Hill. They had to start working fast on an aggressive agenda that would appease their party's loudest, most anti-American factions. This was imperative partly because they wanted to ram as many Democrat agenda items through the system as they could while their party held all the levers of power. But Pelosi and Schumer also knew they could personally lose their own positions of leadership if the Democrats' radical wing decided to go after them for not carrying the banner of radicalism. In many ways, Pelosi and Schumer are hostages to their base, which is rapidly growing away from most Americans.

So, it was no surprise that the first major bills Speaker Pelosi championed in the U.S. House were deeply partisan. This is the only context that explains why—in the midst of a deadly pandemic and worldwide societal shutdowns that left millions of Americans dead, jobless, or homeless—Pelosi's top priority was to pass House of Representatives bill 1 (H.R. 1). This was an election reform bill designed to create a fortification for the permanent election of Democrats. It was cleverly named the "For the People Act." It would have been more accurately called "The Corrupt Politicians Act."

The Democrats then passed a series of bills disguised as COVID-19 relief bills that sought to reward the Democrats' political allies in the state governments and pay off unions and other campaign supporters.

THE CORRUPT POLITICIANS ACT

Speaker Pelosi introduced H.R. 1 on January 4, 2021. For those unfamiliar with congressional customs and traditions, the first bills introduced during a new legislative session serve to set the tone of the leading party's legislative agenda going forward. (In fact, the majority party traditionally reserves the first ten bills that get introduced.) At the time Pelosi introduced H.R. 1, the COVID-19 pandemic was still raging. The first COVID-19 vaccines had been approved for use the month prior, but no one in America had been fully vaccinated. In fact, only 1.5 percent of Americans had received the first dose of a vaccine.[1] Further, the unemployment rate was at 6.3 percent (up from 3.5 percent the year prior and recovering from a staggering 13.3 percent in May 2020).[2] So, as millions of Americans were out of work, grieving for lost loved ones, or battling a deadly virus, the Democrats' highest priority was introducing this bill, which did nothing to help struggling Americans.

Instead, it aimed to centralize power over our nations' elections and give Democrats a lock on future elections. In many ways, H.R. 1 sought to take some of the most contentious election practices of the 2021 election, magnify them, and impose them on the entire country.

If signed into law, H.R. 1 would deeply diminish the constitutional power held by states to administer elections. It would require states to automatically register all eligible residents to vote—whether the residents request it or not. This includes making colleges voter registration centers. If, in this process, the state accidentally adds ineligible people to the rolls—including dead people or noncitizens—the state election officials would face no prosecution for doing so.

Right off the bat, it would erase consequences for states that kept sloppy voter rolls. Furthermore, the bill would make it harder for states to clean their voter rolls of ineligible voters for federal elections. The law would prohibit state election officials from removing voters based on returned, non-forwardable mail or failure to vote in previous elections. Ironically, it would be specifically harder to remove voters who are registered in multiple states, because H.R. 1 would limit states' ability to remove voters based on shared interstate voter registration checks.

The law would also override states' voter identification requirements by mandating that voters could sign sworn affidavits or give the last four digits of their Social Security number in lieu of presenting proof of identification. And it would decree—despite any other state laws—that criminals could vote so long as they weren't currently serving felony sentences.

All of these provisions, coupled with the bill's forced proliferation of by-mail voting, would create an election system that is founded in chaos. Anyone willing to lie to an election worker will be able to cast ballots—in as many precincts as they like. Think about that. Someone who is already willing to break the law by voting in multiple places or under a false name is not likely to have a problem lying on a piece of paper. Further, if someone signs an affidavit with a false name, what is the likelihood that person would ever be found or prosecuted?

As U.S. representative Claudia Tenney (R-NY) wrote for *The Hill* on March 3, 2021:

> "H.R. 1 would prevent election officials from maintaining accurate voter lists and make it harder for them to determine if voters are registered in multiple jurisdictions. This increases the likelihood that voter rolls are outdated and inaccurate or contain ineligible voters."[3]

Basic ballot security will be impossible because there will be no way to verify anything at virtually any part of the system. State officials won't really know who is eligible to vote, because the voter roles will be a mess. Election officials will not know who is voting because there will be no way to verify a voter's identity—either in person or by mail. Elections will become open season for cheaters.

In the name of limiting the influence of money in politics, H.R. 1 seeks to force nonprofits and political organizations that contribute to campaigns or run political ads to release the names of any donors who contribute $10,000 or more to their organizations. Of course, it doesn't matter whether the donors were specifically supporting the ads or campaigns the organizations run. Nor does it matter if they contributed to the organizations in a political context at all. The radical activist Democrats merely want to make sure they can identify and blacklist any American who doesn't support their agenda. Similarly, the bill calls for shareholders of publicly traded companies to be able to find out any political spending by the companies.

These provisions may seem like reasonable efforts to purge so-called "dark money" from our election ecosystem. But they are really power grabs by the activists who want to perpetuate cancel culture as a means of control throughout our society. They want to know who they must silence to get what they want. The free speech and privacy violations in these provisions have even earned H.R. 1 criticism from the American Civil Liberties Union— hardly a conservative institution—although the ACLU supports many of the other provisions in the bill.

Speaking of money and corruption in politics, H.R. 1 calls for the creation of a federal piggy bank for people who want to jump-start their political careers. The bill would establish a 6:1 matching system for U.S. House candidates who only collect small-dollar donations ($200 or less). So, anyone who wants to run for Congress and participates in this program can get $1,200 from the federal government for every $200 the candidate raises from individuals. To qualify, a candidate would have to raise $50,000 on their own from 1,000 individuals before they could tap into the public funds. But provided they could find 1,000 people to give them $50, there is no clear upper limit on how much money one candidate could draw. It's also unclear what the candidate could do with the money if they lost the election. A losing candidate who was able to raise $100,000 in small dollar donations during a given election could get $600,000 in campaign funds from public coffers. They then have $700,000 to give another candidate or pay their friends and families salaries for working on the failed campaign.

The Democrats claim this program would not be funded by taxpayers—instead being funded by diverting fines collected from white-collars criminals. However, the bill doesn't actually establish this funding mechanism—thereby avoiding review from the Congressional Budget Office or other watchdogs.

Perhaps the most insidious effort of Speaker Pelosi's H.R. 1 is the provision that would make the Federal Election Commission a partisan political organ. Currently, the FEC is a nonpartisan, independent federal agency that works to ensure transparency in election campaign funding. It ensures that all candidates—regardless of political party—properly disclose their campaign funding and expenses. It also ensures candidates don't accept money beyond the individual limits for citizens and other organizations. The FEC is one of the few federal agencies that are generally regarded as fair and nonpartisan. However, since September 2019, the body has only had three commissioners and has been unable to meet a quorum to conduct its business.

When fully seated, the FEC is made up of six commissioners—typically three Republicans and three Democrats. Commissioners are appointed by the president of the United States, although law prevents one political party from having majority influence. As the FEC website puts it:

"By law, no more than three Commissioners can represent the same political party, and at least four votes are required for any official Commission action. This structure was created to encourage nonpartisan decisions."[4]

In H.R. 1, Pelosi seeks to make the FEC a partisan body, by limiting the number of commissioners to five, giving the party in power an extra seat at the table. This will effectively weaponize the FEC to be a campaign finance enforcement arm on behalf of whatever political party holds power in Washington. This effort to politicize the FEC has nothing to do with election integrity, bipartisanship, or any other virtuous effort. It is purely a political power grab.

This is why no Republicans voted for this bill—and why all but one Democrat voted for it. (Democratic representative Bennie G. Thompson voted against the bill, saying his constituents did not want campaigns to be financed with public funds or the bill's prescribed redistricting scheme.)[5] The final vote in the U.S. House was 220–210.

As Republican Leader Kevin McCarthy said of the Democrats' first bill, "Democrats call H.R. 1 the 'For the People Act.' But it's really a 'For the Politicians Act.' It's not designed to protect your vote. It's designed to put a thumb on the scale of every election in America and keep the swamp swampy."[6]

As I'm writing this, H.R. 1 is stalled in the U.S. Senate, because no Republican will support it—nor will West Virginia's Democratic senator Joe Manchin.

Finally, outside of Washington, D.C., this effort to federalize elections is deeply opposed. Specifically, according to nationwide surveys by McLaughlin & Associates in February 2021, 81 percent of Americans believe people should have to show photo identification to vote. Further, 85 percent support signature verification for any mail-in votes.

THE COVID-19 SPENDING SPREE

In addition to H.R. 1, Congressional Democrats helped deliver a $1.9 trillion giveaway to their political allies and supporters.

President Biden's so-called "American Rescue Plan" became law on March 11, 2021. While it was hailed as yet another COVID-19 relief bill, less than 10 percent of the $1.9 trillion in the spending package was dedicated to fighting the spread of the virus, treating people infected with it, or on public health efforts in general. Most of the remainder was devoted to paying off unions and other Democrat allies who support Democratic campaigns, bailing out states that have been run into the ground by decades of big-government Democrat leaders, and a laundry list of various left-wing pet projects that would infuriate most Americans if they were honestly reported.

As the Heritage Foundation's Matthew D. Dickerson wrote in *The National Interest*:

"For example, nearly $90 billion is earmarked for a taxpayer-funded bailout of union pension plans that were massively underfunded long before [COVID-19]. This union bailout gets about twice as much funding as COVID-19 testing and contact tracing.

"The bill would provide $126 billion for K–12 schools around the country. But the non-partisan Congressional Budget Office says that only $6.2 billion of that—just five percent—would actually be spent by October. More of this funding will be spent in 2026 than in 2021. How is that supposed to help reopen our schools?

"The bill," Dickerson wrote, "would send another $350 billion to state and local governments, on top of the hundreds of billions already provided. This spending is completely unwarranted, as last year's coronavirus relief measures have already given states windfall funding well in excess of their projected revenue shortfalls. Worse, this round of bailouts will reward those states that enacted especially draconian lockdowns that wrecked their economies, closing businesses and pushing workers onto unemployment."[7]

Every American should be infuriated at this $1.9 trillion giveaway. In the spirit of Hillary Clinton and Rahm Emanuel, the Democrats didn't let the crisis of COVID-19 "go to waste." They used it as a way to reward political allies and secure future support. (Of course, they also made sure to include another round of stimulus checks to blunt the public's anger.)

The Democrats' second-wave spending bonanza was Biden's $2 trillion infrastructure package. As I said at the time, this proposal is a tax increase, masquerading as an infrastructure bill, masquerading as a jobs bill. Democrats again gave it a pleasant, clever title:

"The American Jobs Plan." But it should be called the "American Job Killing Tax Plan." Rather than create jobs and build up our decaying infrastructure, this plan will destroy jobs and cause infrastructure projects to be more costly in time and money.

A key provision in the American Job Killing Tax Plan would increase corporate taxes by one-third, from 21 percent to 28 percent. It would also establish a minimum 21 percent tax rate for multinational U.S. corporations and hike taxes on oil and gas companies—which will lead to higher costs for fuel, heating oil, asphalt, and plastic. When companies have to pay higher taxes, they cannot afford to hire more employees. When major multinational corporations get charged steep taxes by the United States, they move their headquarters out of the United States. When petroleum products cost more money, infrastructure projects cost more money.

Raising taxes is the single worst thing you can do if you want to spur job creation. As Travis Nix wrote for *The National Review*:

> "The plan would increase the corporate-tax rate to 28 percent, which would be the highest in the world, and it would increase the global minimum tax on American companies' foreign earnings. Together, these changes would tank America's ability to compete with other nations, increase the probability of companies' shifting jobs overseas, and destroy incentives for businesses to make the job-growing and wage-growing investments that strengthen the economy.
>
> "Increasing corporate taxes by 7 percentage points would kneecap the United States' ability to compete with its biggest rivals. Including state taxes, America would have

a 32.34 percent statutory corporate-tax rate. This would be the highest in the Organization for Economic Cooperation and Development (OECD). The U.S. corporate-tax rate would be greater even than Communist China's. Under this plan, companies would undoubtedly choose to invest overseas instead of being burdened with Biden's sky-high taxes, and American workers would lose."[8]

Setting the job killing tax increases aside, others have criticized the plan because it has little to do with infrastructure. The largest tranches of spending in the plan go to child and elderly care (roughly $400 billion) and affordable housing ($213 billion). Most Americans would not list these two categories as traditional infrastructure—roads, bridges, waterways, and energy grids. Further, there are already ample federal programs to support these areas.

As Richard A. Epstein wrote on April 5, 2021, for the Hoover Institution, "They increase the motivation to stay out of the workforce, in fact, and thereby reduce the size of the tax base as overall expenditures are mushrooming. Moreover, large doses of home/community care are difficult to target exclusively to the needy. A correct analysis seeks to determine whether such payments are directed toward the truly needy and whether they induce people to leave the workforce to become tax recipients rather than taxpayers."[9]

Further, the focus on affordable housing appears to be President Biden again picking up the Democrat effort to federalize local zoning laws and begin to forcibly urbanize suburbs across the nation by doing away with single-family home zoning. This has become a staple in the Democrats' playbook—and a clear example of Washington politicians ignoring their own dictates. As Betsy McCaughey wrote in the *New York Post*:

> "The Biden plan's backers are hypocrites. Biden himself owns a four-acre lakefront home in upscale Greenville, Del., where there is absolutely no public housing, afford-able housing or rentals that accept housing vouchers. And don't expect any to be built next door to the Bidens."[10]

To add insult to injury, at the time Biden's $1.9 trillion bill was passed, there was already $1 trillion in real COVID-19 relief that had still not been spent. At the time I'm writing this in the middle of 2021, the Committee for a Responsible Budget's COVID Money Tracker reports there is presently $5.4 trillion of federal COVID-19 relief funding that has not been spent. The federal deficit is expected to reach $3.4 trillion this year—a staggering and shameful record.

If this radical spending spree isn't stopped, the Biden admin-istration will rack up a bill that will be simply too steep to pay.

FRENCH HISTORY LESSONS FOR PELOSI AND SCHUMER

History has a cautionary tale for Pelosi, Schumer, and virtually every establishment Democrat. In addition to losing control of the House—and potentially the Senate—they should be concerned about the state of their own party. The radical wing of the party is growing rapidly and being championed by the media, Big Tech, and academia. If the Democrats suddenly find themselves in the minority, this energized left wing may turn its hostility toward the party's leadership.

In this way, Pelosi and Schumer could learn something from the French Revolution. In fact, the terms "Left" and "Right" earned their political meanings during the French Revolution. Those who opposed the monarchy sat to the left of the president's chair in the French National Assembly. Those who supported the monarchy sat to the right. Many people think of the French and American revolutions as being inspired by the same ideas. Both groups of revolutionaries used similar language—equality, rights, liberty—but they meant very different things by those terms.

The Jacobins, Montagnards, and several of the left-wing factions behind the French Revolution weren't just trying to replace what they saw as a tyrannical government. They wanted to tear down all elements of the past that influenced human behavior. The French left believed they needed a blank slate to achieve a perfect society. They even went so far as to decree that January 1, 1789, was the beginning of history.

Today, Pelosi and Schumer are presiding over a party that is increasingly being taken over by modern-day Jacobins. This spirit of rewriting history to impose a new ideology is being carried out by the members of the woke left who want to vilify our Founders, erase our founding documents, revise our history, and silence anyone who opposes their ideology.

In addition to being anti-monarchy, the French Revolution movement was also virulently anti-Catholic. Its leaders aimed to eliminate God because religion represented a source of authority other than the pure reason of the country's enlightened intellectuals. The leaders of the American Revolution, however, believed that God was the source of all rights, and that a republican form of government could not survive without virtuous people.

Again, today, we see the Democratic left regularly attacking religious beliefs and figures as bigoted, primitive, and unfit for modern society. Instead, the Democrats uplift their own elites and experts as moral authorities over religious institutions. Consider how congregations at churches and synagogues were shamed—and in some cases fined—for breaking COVID-19 shutdown rules in so-called progressive states. Orthodox Jews in New York were consistently shamed, ridiculed, and locked out of synagogues by Governor Andrew Cuomo and Mayor Bill de Blasio. In Nevada, for example, the secular state health officials enforced limits on the size of religious gatherings but did not impose the same rules on casinos or secular businesses. The Ninth Circuit Court of Appeals later found the state's selective treatment of churches unconstitutional.[11]

The French Revolution was also deeply hostile to class differences and wealth. In France, almost 90 percent of the population was made up of the peasant class, and the divide between the rich and the poor was a function of birth rather than merit. The revolutionaries were contemptuous of the customs and ceremonies of aristocratic life. This hostility led to a concept of egalitarianism focused on group rights—an equality of ends—achieved through individual responsibilities to the whole as expressed through the government's actions.

America, meanwhile, was a far less stratified society. With the clearly notable exception of slavery, the colonies enjoyed a great deal of social mobility. There was an aristocratic class, but there was a general belief that people could escape poverty through hard work and determination. Thus, the American concept of equality was grounded in individual rights, not the rights of a group. The American Founders believed people must be treated equally under the law, not made equal by it.

Today's Democrats, whom Pelosi and Schumer have to lead, are explicitly combating the notion that one can break out of poverty by working hard. Instead, the woke left says systemic oppression exists at every turn to keep people beneath "the one percent." The American mythos of belt-tightening and pulling oneself up from one's bootstraps is a lie, they say. The woke left constantly highlights and complains about divisions in our society—then actively organizes and promotes these divisions.

The catch-22 of left-wing governance is that focusing on group rights instead of individual ones—and imposing an equality of ends rather than equality under the law—requires a privileged ruling class running a powerful central government to impose sameness on everyone. The quest for perfect, forced equality always leads to deep inequality and tyranny. The danger is compounded when the powerful ruling class rejects traditional morality and takes license to do anything to achieve its goals.

These differences in belief over equality, rights, and morality in society is why the American and French revolutions—despite sharing similar themes—produced vastly different results.

The American Revolution was the foundation for free markets, representative democracy, and individual liberty. The French Revolution was the foundation for communism, socialism, and fascism.

The American Revolution resulted in the Articles of Confederation, which were later peacefully replaced with the U.S.

Constitution. The document remains the longest surviving charter of government in the world today. The French Revolution resulted in complete chaos.

For the first few years of the French Revolution, the anti-monarchists had the majority, and they eventually succeeded in dissolving the monarchy. However, the increasing radicalism of the left in the National Convention (the successor to the National Assembly) began to alienate moderates who mostly represented rural areas outside of Paris. A counterrevolutionary revolt began.

The French left reacted by neutering the power of the whole legislative body and concentrating power into a few small committees. So, after toppling a monarchy, they created a dictatorship. This dictatorship enacted what became known as a "reign of terror." Tens of thousands of people were executed after being judged enemies of the revolution in phony trials. Then, the leaders behind the terror were themselves executed, and a series of riots and counterterrors led to the adoption of a more moderate constitution in 1795.

This is the key lesson for Pelosi and Schumer. It's only a matter of time before the woke radicals turn inward and decide the current Democratic Party isn't pure enough. Pelosi and Schumer must be concerned about losing the already eroding moderate wing in the Democrat Party. Increasingly, these members will be challenged in primaries (and defeated) by the growing radical, woke wing, which has far more energy and enthusiasm. Once that happens, Pelosi and Schumer could be next on the (figurative) chopping block.

As for Americans who support today's radical woke movement: there are other important lessons to learn from the French Revolution.

After its initial revolutionary leaders were executed, France arrived at its third form of government in five years. Even this constitution failed to produce a stable government. Napoleon Bonaparte abolished the legislative body in a coup d'état in 1799 and was declared emperor in 1804.

After fifteen years of riots, executions, and famine, France ended up with a monarchy again but with an emperor instead of a king.

Despite the French Revolution's record of failure and misery, the modern American left's goal is still to replace equality under the law and traditional morality with the equality of results and the primacy of human reason over faith and tradition.

Just like the left of the French revolution, the American left attacks the rich—"the 1 percent"—and its solution to income inequality is still forced wealth redistribution rather than a more dynamic economy that can support better-paying jobs for all. They still fight against the essential role of religion and tradition in creating a virtuous people capable of self-government. That is why the Democrats fight so bitterly for abortion, against traditional marriage, and against the teaching of American history in a way that validates our founding generation.

Most of all, the American left still supports empowering a ruling class of bureaucrats and intellectuals to micromanage our lives and impose its vision of ideal society on America. That is why the left supports the continued expansion of government into health care, education, our food supply, the marketplace, and all other vital areas of our economy.

However, the good news is: modern America is not revolutionary France. If the most radical elements of the American left consume the Democratic Party, all the polling and surveys

I have seen indicate radicalism will simply be rejected by the American majority.

The bottom line: whether it is because of forces within their own party or the will of the American majority, Schumer's and Pelosi's days in leadership are numbered. They know this. It helps explain their desperate effort to grab power.

CHAPTER FOUR

HOW WE GOT HERE

The radical Democrats would like us to believe that we have now come through the last great election, and after the 2020 election the future belongs to them. This is not true. We are in a series of electoral and governmental shocks, and the excitement has only just begun.

Let me explain by taking a slight detour into recent history.

The nomination and election of Donald J. Trump in 2016 was an enormous shock to the political system and especially to the elites who had been dominating it for the last eighty-nine years. Trump's defeat of Hillary Clinton deepened this shock to the elites' system. The people who four years later would demand an immediate acceptance of Joe Biden as president fully rejected the Trump victory for his entire presidency. His election was a profound upset to their old order.

As part of our unpredicted and unpredictable journey during the Trump years, the eruption of the Chinese virus was the most powerful single disrupter. Pre-COVID-19, the economy was booming. We had the lowest Black and Latino unemployment in history. Women outnumbered men in the U.S. workforce. Real median household income had risen from $62,898 in 2016 to $68,703 in 2019—a record high.[1] Trump's reelection seemed likely, if not inevitable.

Then came a pandemic that crippled the economy, gave local and state governments absurdly dictatorial levels of power, exposed the confusion and dishonesty of public health services, and isolated people through lockdowns. As the news media constantly waxed hysterical, virtually everyone seemed threatened with death. As the national leader during COVID-19, Trump ultimately came to personify a response that seemed too late, too confused, too disorganized, and too abrasive. The fact is whatever President Trump did is going to be judged harshly by the elites. They saw their opportunity to destroy their mortal enemy, and they took it. They did not allow facts, fairness, or decency to slow them down.

But the previous four years were remarkably dynamic and different from the America norm. The rise of Trump was an enormous change from the gradual bureaucratic decay of previous years. When I published *Trump and the American Future: Solving the Great Problems of Our Time* in June 2020, I was convinced America had a deeply optimistic future (in the immediate sense).

To some extent, I was still caught up in the euphoria of February 2020, when the already strong economy was still building momentum. Normally, a booming economy was a good sign for an incumbent president. The polls indicated President Trump was making real inroads into both the African American and Latino communities. Everything seemed on track for a Trump second term. The crowds for the president were enormous and enthusiastic wherever he went. To see how we could have missed the signs of trouble, go back and look at Biden's frightened, COVID-19-dominated, drive-in mini-rallies, campaigning from the basement, and then look at the scale of the Trump rallies.

Given the sense of optimism, I began to work on a visionary positive agenda for a Trump second term. With the help of our great team at Gingrich 360, we developed a positive book with a lot of opportunities to build on the many breakthroughs in taxes, regulations, trade agreements, and a steady focus on American interests, American values, and American history.

And then along came the Chinese virus (as it was accurately, but politically incorrectly, termed). We should have known how tough the summer and fall would be. We should have looked at how hard the news media had worked since late 2016 to smear, attack, distort, and lie about President Trump. I had been actively studying and working on politics and government since August 1958. Never in sixty-two years had I seen the kind of ferocity and dishonesty that defined the media's reaction to the entire Trump presidency (something that goes on to this day as many Trump administration staffers find themselves canceled and barred from opportunities—and blocked from any hope of reentering mainstream American life).

It wasn't that I was unaware of how tough politics and self-government could be. My early days in Georgia were a real introduction to the willingness of an elite system to use every tool possible to sustain itself in power against a new generation of reformers. I was a Pennsylvania-born army brat who had grown up in an integrated United States Army. I came to Georgia in February of my junior year in high school when my father was assigned to Fort Benning.

Georgia in 1960 was a one-party state. It was controlled by segregationist Democrats quite willing to use the force of government to sustain segregation and crush those who advocated integration. To openly advocate the end of the Democratic Party's imposition of segregation was to risk a burning cross in your yard (as happened to one of the Republican leaders, Rodney Cook).

Segregationist Democrats maintained their position of dominating African Americans by a combination of force (both government and private), demagoguery, and direct personal intimidation—losing your job, having your family threatened, and being cut off economically and politically. Using vicious language, describing people in nasty terms, and being prepared to imprison, beat up, and in some cases kill opponents of segregation was seen as the unpleasant but unavoidable cost of keeping the white community dominant and the Black community subservient.

All of the techniques segregationist Democrats were using in the early 1960s have now evolved into the techniques the new racist woke Democrats are using today. Consider the astonishing parallels. Segregationist mobs used violence to intimidate opponents of the system. Today, woke mobs, advocates for Black Lives Matter, and Antifa use violence to impose their agenda—this includes burning buildings, looting stores, and physically attacking people.

Segregationist legislatures and school boards fired teachers who broke ranks and advocated the end of segregation. Today it is the colleges, universities, and teachers' unions who provide the policing that guarantees little or no dissent in the classroom against the tenets of the woke order. Those who don't understand the new orthodoxy are driven from their careers. The weirdest things can be advocated by those on the left with little or no negative consequences. Yet, any questioning of the woke orthodoxy can lead to ostracism, firing, and lawsuits.

Like most Americans, I thought we were beyond the brutal, terrorizing, cultural, legal and political warfare that the South had suffered from for a generation—and which the left sought to impose on the country in the late 1960s. The election of 2016 and its aftermath proved us spectacularly naive and wrong.

THE ESTABLISHMENT STRIKES BACK

When candidate Trump defeated fifteen other Republicans to win the Republican nomination in 2016, I thought it was both an amazing tribute to his skills, his understanding of marketing, and the degree to which he was willing to say what he really believed without regard to the news media or the pollsters. Candidate Trump was a man on a mission, and he came across like one.

Trump's nomination was also a sign of the almost total repudiation of the Washington Republican establishment. When he began his race, 63 percent of Republicans told pollsters they did not like the Republican establishment in Washington. It was almost the kiss of death for Trump's competitors during the primary to admit they had worked in Washington.

The degree to which Trump was able to reunify the party by the Republican National Convention was remarkable. He was a genuine outsider who had engaged in what in corporate terms would have been called a hostile takeover. He campaigned directly against the wars and the trade policies that had been the proud achievements of the last two Republican presidents. He mocked their failures in trade negotiations. The GOP establishment, which had never agreed with President Ronald Reagan, found itself positively loathing candidate Trump. They hated his policies, tone, style, coarse language, and non–Ivy League academic background (Wharton School did not count to them). For the Republican establishment, it was as though the Clampetts had seized power, and the Beverly Hillbillies had taken over "their" party, which they had been running for nearly three decades.

Despite all this, Republican National Committee chairman Reince Priebus had held the party together, and the Trump team used the convention to build on their primary victories and unify the GOP. They were helped in reuniting the GOP by the specter of a Clinton presidency. I am not sure candidate Trump could have defeated anyone other than former secretary of state Clinton. She had a unique set of weaknesses that brought together a remarkable coalition of "anyone but Hillary." Because of his brilliant performance and organizational skills, Trump turned out to be the "anyone."

Clinton carried the scars of her husband's eight years in office. While the relationship with Monica Lewinsky was a major problem for Republicans and some independents, it was not the greatest burden Secretary Clinton was forced to carry as a candidate. Secretary Clinton carried three huge challenges going into 2007—and again running in 2016. They proved insurmountable both against Obama in 2008 and then against Trump in 2016.

Matt Bai wrote a remarkable book, *The Argument: Inside the Battle to Remake Democratic Politics,* about the Democratic Party in 2005–06. Bai suggested that the assumption that Hillary was inevitable in 2008 was entirely a Washington phenomenon. Bai crisscrossed the country in 2005 and 2006. He visited Democratic

Party meetings, dinners, and rallies. He visited with left-wing activist groups who disdained the traditional party structure. He visited elected Democrats and the consultants, pollsters, and analysts who provided their support systems. Finally, Bai went to the monied donors who were funding the party.

Everywhere he went, Bai found deep unhappiness. The party faithful believed they had defeated George W. Bush in 2000 and that in 2004, a ruthless Karl Rove–designed campaign had lied about their nominee, Senator John Kerry. They were frustrated by the narrow 2004 defeat in a race they believed they had won. I had been invited to an overwhelmingly liberal Democratic news media luncheon on election day 2004. The conversation assumed Bush was gone. In fact, one of the luncheon guests clearly thought they would become the next secretary of state, and the news media members openly discussed what the takeover at the State Department would be like in the new Kerry administration. The exit polls indicated a Kerry victory and a decisive defeat of President Bush. In retrospect, it is strange how parallel the emotions of impending victory were for Democrats in 2004 and 2016.

Furthermore, the left was deeply offended by the thought of another Clinton presidency. Their complaint was that the Clintons had sold out liberalism by governing from the center in partnership with congressional Republicans. The very triangulation that Dick Morris invented, and which may have enabled President Clinton to get reelected in 1996, was a deep insult to the progressive wing of the Democratic Party. They wanted a president who fought for their values and their programs. They were infuriated that Clinton was selling them out for his own ambitions. Reforming welfare, balancing the budget for four straight years, accelerating economic growth through the largest capital gains tax cut in history, and a host of other reforms got Bill Clinton reelected but put an enormous burden on his wife's future hopes of becoming president.

Just as the Republican grass roots was fed up with its Washington leadership in 2015, the Democratic activists a decade earlier were adamant about the need for a new leader who could combine the left's ideology with an attractive approach capable of reaching independents and moderate Republicans on progressive terms. In this new world, Hillary was trapped into being the aging insider. She had been around too long. She had been in Washington too long. The Democratic grassroots revolution occurred in 2007 and 2008. Barack Obama rode the outsider wave in that cycle fully as much as Trump would among Republicans eight years later.

During those eight Obama years, grassroots Republicans and conservative activists grew more alienated from the Washington-based old Republican Party. The Tea Party movement and its congressional corollary, the Freedom Caucus, were direct reflections of the grassroots frustration with a liberal President Obama masquerading as a moderate and seeming to dance around the Republican leaders who simply proved to be incapable of keeping up with the audacious, bold, and ambitious Democratic president.

During the Obama years, Hillary Clinton became more of an insider—even as the American people got more fed up with the establishment in both parties. There may be no position in government more distant from the American people than secretary of state. If Hillary planned to run again for president, there could be no job less likely to be a springboard to the White House. The secretary of state had to focus overseas. Given the multilateralism and globalism inherent in Obama's worldview, being his secretary of state was bound to irritate and alienate a lot of Americans. Tragic events such as the killing of the American ambassador in Benghazi, Libya, further weakened Secretary Clinton with the American people.

In addition to having lost the trust of the progressives—and having become an insider in an age of hunger for outsiders—Hillary had one other really big problem. She was simply unlikable. All the charm and love of people in the Clinton family came from Bill. Both he and Obama could light up an audience with their smiles. Both could charm their opponents by paying attention to them. Hillary could not light up a room even if you built a bonfire for her. She was the gloomy, determined, hardworking grind who did well by simply outworking everyone else. It was a terrible burden for a candidate to carry.

All this was compounded by the weird scandal of the missing emails, the destruction of hard drives, and the host of still unexplained activities that would have historically blown into a scandal comparable to President Richard Nixon and Watergate—but somehow due to news media bias and FBI protection magically just simmered along, weakening her candidacy but not destroying it.

Despite all these weaknesses, Hillary was still a contender in the fall of 2015. This was largely due to the different—but equally severe—weaknesses of her opponent, candidate Trump. Trump in 2016 had the weaknesses of his strengths. He had unimaginable belief in his own knowledge, intuition, and skills. When he was right, he was historic (and history has literally been changed by his insights and courage). However, when he was wrong, he was as wrong as when he was right. Furthermore, because all this was occurring within his own mind, he had no natural systems for self-correction or seeking serious advice.

Trump turned the tweet into a tool as powerful as President Franklin D. Roosevelt's fireside chats on radio. His large Twitter and Facebook followings combined with his instinct for the ruthlessly powerful attack enabled him to fight virtually the entire news media to a standstill. Indeed, you could argue that among American presidents only Andrew Jackson, Abraham Lincoln, and FDR were capable of this kind of all-out communications fight with the entire national establishment.

Trump intuited the concerns and beliefs of working Americans and their families to an amazing degree. His natural parallel was the late Rush Limbaugh. Both Trump and Limbaugh had a knack of understanding the American people and putting into words what they were thinking but were unable to articulate themselves. Also, like Limbaugh, Trump's courage, authenticity, and understanding of mass audiences was unrivaled. He had *The Apprentice* TV show for years. His work with Miss Universe, Trump hotels and golf courses, and merchandising various products made him possibly the most consumer-oriented president in our history. Importantly, he understood that consumers and voters were the same people.

He was incredibly successful as an outsider. And yet . . .

There is an enormous difficulty in being a true outsider. Every mistake will be magnified. Every nuance or lack of clarity will be held against you. The strength of the heroic outsider is connected to the conditions that make it difficult to survive. In this sense, Candidate and then President Trump could be compared to Greek and Nordic heroes who are more than human and yet have tragic flaws that doom them because of their greatness.

Trump was hammered by a bunch of blows during the fall 2016 campaign of which the *Access Hollywood* tape may have been the most dangerous and damaging. Yet, his great strength was that he never flinched or backed down. He fought his way through every attack. There was no defense. It was all offense. No traditional consultant could have imagined the ferocity, intelligence, and skills of Trump's fall campaign in 2016. As an example: when Clinton wanted to bring up the issue of Trump's sex life in the debate, Trump invited to the debate all the women who had attacked her husband as a predator. That debate should be a must-watch for any class on debating. The American people wanted authenticity, toughness, audacity, and a willingness to fight no matter how tough things became. Trump could deliver that. Hillary could not.

The last great factor in the 2016 campaign was Trump's ability to understand the actual rules for electing presidents. In a sense this was the most ironic advantage of all. Here was Hillary Clinton, trained at Yale Law School, and a professional politician at least since the 1972 McGovern campaign if not longer. She was married to another Yale-educated lawyer who had been attorney general for his state. She was surrounded by an entire army of smart, ruthless professionals—and they forgot the most basic ground rule for becoming president of the United States. Under the U.S. Constitution, presidents are elected by states—not by popular majorities. It may have been a comment on the left's contempt for the Constitution that Hillary's team simply forgot this most basic rule in presidential politics. Trump, as a smart businessman, had spent his lifetime looking carefully at deal language. He knew exactly how you win the presidency. One state at a time.

The radical difference in these two strategies hit me in early October 2016. I was reading articles on polling results, which always began with Hillary's big national lead. Then the reporters would focus on the huge margins for her in California, New York, and other supposedly key states. Suddenly, it hit me that there was an anomaly in the data.

If Hillary was that dramatically ahead in California and New York, then there would be a lot of running room for Trump in the secondary states. That is exactly what was happening. The Trump team was focusing its candidate's time, energy, and resources on the small number of states that would define the election.

However, the nature of the Clinton team's media self-deception caused an enormous problem for the Clinton team (which included most of the news media) and for the Trump team. The Clinton senior management started the evening of the election icing the champagne and getting ready for a great victory they had been working on for several decades. Yet here they were in mid-evening beginning to realize that their candidate was going to lose.

Hillary Clinton is a tough professional. She had been reassured by her staff that everything was fine, and she was going to be the next president. Now someone had to walk in and say it wasn't going to happen.

None of her senior staff wanted to be the bearers of such traumatically terrible news. They needed a good sound explanation of what had gone wrong. It was not possible to imagine that someone incorrigible like Donald Trump could have been chosen by the American people. There had to be another explanation. Time was short. Hillary was demanding answers from her senior staff.

Suddenly, they figured out how to appease Hillary. There was a certain grand irony in that the Russia dossier against Trump we now know was paid for by the Clinton campaign and the Democratic National Committee. We also now know that the dossier was full of misinformation, untruths, and propaganda. But, because it was damaging to President Trump, the establishment media embraced it and spread its lies without a moment of due diligence or traditional journalistic inquiry. In perfect execution of a Saul Alinsky rule for radicalism, the Democrats accused Trump of doing exactly what they were doing—colluding with foreign agents to influence the American election (remember, the dossier was compiled by a former British intelligence agent and sourced from Russian contacts). It was probably not a coincidence that as a young professional Hillary Clinton had counted Alinsky as one of her friends and mentors. They were both Chicagoans and Hillary would meet with him and learn from him while writing her thesis.

Fifty years from now, historians will describe the scale of the Clinton–national establishment lies about Trump as a turning point that ultimately destroyed the American left. The scale of dishonesty, the degree to which it permeated the news media, the degree to which the Justice Department and the Federal Bureau of Investigation seemed corrupted and biased in their handling of both the Clinton and Trump cases—all these steps began to convince conservative Americans that the system was cheating in ways that threatened the very fabric of the system.

While Secretary Clinton personally conceded defeat the day after the election, the radical Democrats rejected her appeal that "we owe Donald Trump an open mind and a chance to lead." In fact, the left had begun to respond to the threat of a Trump victory by openly discussing impeachment before the election. The day after the election, there were already mobilization meetings in eight cities. The day of the Trump inauguration *The Washington Post* had a story on potential impeachment. The day after the inauguration there was a massive women's rally on the National Mall of left-wing activists pledging to defeat the Trump presidency. At that rally, the singer Madonna explained "Yes, I'm angry." She went on to say, "Yes, I'm outraged. Yes, I have thought an awful lot about blowing up the White House."

Beyond Madonna the amazing part about the Women's March was that it started on social media the day after the election and spread like wildfire. Ultimately, there were events in all fifty states and forty foreign countries, with an estimated 4.1 million people at the American rallies.

Thus, President Trump was confronted with an active, militant, and sometimes threatening opposition by the first days of the new administration. This unending four-year assault had several severe consequences that would radically change the trajectory of American politics and government from anything that could have been imagined in the summer of 2016.

First, in their desperate fear and loathing (to borrow from Hunter S. Thompson's book title) about Trump, any lie was acceptable, and any smear was laudable. The larger narrative of saving America from President Trump dwarfed the facts. For example, both *The New York Times* and *The Washington Post* won

Pulitzer Prizes for stories about the alleged Russian collusion in the 2016 election that we now know were totally fabricated.

The fear and loathing went beyond the news media and the elected Democrats to large parts of the federal bureaucracy. Departments such as State and Judiciary (whose employees had given 97 percent to 99 percent of their political donations to Hillary Clinton) became centers of internal resistance.[2] Whenever possible, these bureaucrats stopped and radically slowed Trump initiatives and leaked real and imagined stories to cripple or undermine the duly elected president.

Silicon Valley became a center of fear and loathing to such a degree that Twitter and Facebook became active opponents, censoring and blacking out pro-Trump or anti-Biden activities. If you had told me that America's oldest (and fourth largest) newspaper, the *New York Post*, could be censored by the internet giants with no consequences, I would have thought it impossible. If you had told me that a political leader who received 75 million votes could be erased online by these internet giants, I would have thought it was something that might happen in Communist China or Russia but was unthinkable in America. The pressure cooker of the assault on Trump was changing American patterns and crippling American freedom at a frightening rate. The fear and loathing coalesced the American business elites into an anti-Trump, pro-Biden pattern that is bringing to bear enormous pressure on everyday Americans.

And yet . . .

Despite all the pressures from the elites, the American majority has become even more anti-left, anti-socialist, anti-woke, and anti-cancel culture than they were under Trump. We have a much bigger advantage in the cultural fight than the political fight. Consider this recent polling data from McLaughlin & Associates on key values and issues:

When asked which is the more important federal policy, 59 percent of Americans favored encouraging people who are in need to work and be less dependent on government. Only 32.6 percent said taking care of people in need even regardless of their dependence on government was more important.

By 87.2 percent to 8.3 percent, people favored primarily thinking of themselves as Americans over persons of color. The breakdown was 82.7 percent to 13.8 percent when "ethnicity or background" was substituted for "person of color."

In early 2021, 90 percent of Americans wanted everyone who entered the country illegally to be tested for COVID-19. This included 92 percent of Latinos. At the same time, 75 percent of Americans oppose taxpayer-funded giveaways for people in the country illegally.

Eighty percent want to fully fund police departments in America—this includes 57 percent of African Americans and 70 percent of Latinos. In fact, 72 percent favor mandatory prison sentences for anyone who attacks a police officer.

In response to the radical Democrats' government-run health care—or Medicare-for-All—89 percent of Americans favor consumer choice and private sector competition as the best way to lower drug prices. Further, 85 percent favor lowering health insurance premiums through more consumer choice and private sector competition.

A few others that may surprise you: 72 percent of Americans favor banning abortions after twenty weeks; 75 percent favor antitrust laws for the big internet giants; and 75 percent want to maximize the production of American oil and natural gas.

Consider these results—and think about how Biden and the Democrats are stuck in tiny minorities by their partisan ultra-left base.

This gap between the American majority and the Democrats will only grow as Democrats move further toward radicalism.

PART II

REBUILDING
THE AMERICA
WE LOVE

CHAPTER FIVE

REFORMING TO ENSURE FREE, FAIR, SECURE ELECTIONS

E very serious historian and political scientist should study the 2020 election cycle. It was deeply divisive. It surfaced fierce mistrust and skepticism in our election systems and officials—on both sides of the political aisles. And 2020 was the largest, most active election cycle in our country's history—based on the number and percentage of people who voted. The size was particularly remarkable given that the elections were held during a historic global pandemic. So, purely from the magnitude, it was historic.

According to the U.S. Census Bureau, 67 percent of all adult U.S. citizens cast ballots in 2020. This was up 5 percent from 2016. Turnout hit records for nearly every ethnic demographic—the only exception being Black voters, who voted in higher numbers in President Obama's elections in 2008 (65 percent) and 2012 (67 percent) than in 2020 (63 percent). Every age group also turned out in record numbers.[1]

The figures were high because the 2020 elections were probably the most accessible elections we have ever held. This was due to the widespread lifting of restrictions for mail-in absentee ballots, loosening of voting deadlines, relaxing signature and ballot verification processes, expanding public ballot drop-off points, and other administrative changes in states and precincts across the country. It is also probably true that more total money was spent in a wider range of creative ways than any election since the Bryan-McKinley election of 1896 (about which Karl Rove wrote a brilliant study: *The Triumph of William McKinley: Why the Election of 1896 Still Matters*).

Of course, these major changes; a passionate, almost rabid desire to beat President Trump; and a realization that the rules changes made to mitigate the impact of the COVID-19 pandemic on voting also spurred a great deal of questions. People were rightly concerned over the integrity of our elections, ballot security, and the importance of upholding state laws (in several states, election processes were changed outside what state law appeared to allow). The election changes, the skepticism, the media's vehement condemnation of anyone who raised concerns about the integrity of the elections, and President Trump's insistence that there was fraud in the election created an atmosphere that elevated normal partisan sniping to unprecedented hostility. All of this reached a terrible crescendo on January 6, 2021, as a frenzied mob stormed the U.S. Capitol Building and sought to disrupt Congress from certifying the 2020 election. All the various agents of the radical left insisted that responsibility for the January 6 attack fell solely on President Trump, but they were either ignorant of reality or intentionally deflecting blame.

First, responsibility for the attack belongs solely to the people who treasonously broke into the Capitol—and no one else. However, responsibility for the environment that led to the attack belongs to everyone who helped it along. This includes every election official who changed the rules of the elections without authority, every person who made accusations of fraud without proof, every member of the media and Big Tech who silenced stories about legitimate concerns, and every activist who fought against commonsense election security measures in the name of imaginary vote suppression.

In a less direct way, this environment of mistrust and hostility was also fueled by the months of protests and riots that had begun in the summer of 2020 over the death of George Floyd and other Black men who were killed by police. To be sure, there were peaceful demonstrations at the time. But there was also real and serious violence in cities across the nation that left homes and businesses burned, people harmed, and stores looted. Violence boiled in Portland, Oregon, for a year. A portion of Seattle, Washington, surrounding a police precinct was abandoned by the government for months as radical vandals took it over. Shootings in cities such as Chicago skyrocketed as police were increasingly intimidated from doing their jobs and hamstrung by their local officials. All the while, the national media reported on fires, looting, and violence but constantly refrained that the social justice protests were "mostly peaceful." This perpetually sustained lie created dissonance and eroded the trust millions of Americans had in our societal institutions leading up to the elections. By the fall, tension had reached the point of snapping and the level of mistrust was insurmountable.

People on both sides of the political spectrum were wound up. They were brimming with certainty of their virtue thanks to our various, carefully cultivated echo chambers, and they were conditioned to an us-vs.-them mindset. Once the election came around, it was easy for the left to convince its side that all Republicans were racists desperately seeking to suppress minority voting. And people on the right were ready to accept that everyone on the left was trying to steal the election. There was no middle ground or room for debate. The paradigm was established. Retrospectively examining this model, it is easy to see how the January 6 attack happened—even though it was completely unbelievable in the moment.

My goal here is not to relitigate this sad, dark moment of American history. It is to help prevent something like it from happening again. To this end, I worry that as bad as the 2020 election madness was, the 2024 elections could be even worse—unless Americans (Republicans and Democrats) at every level of society can come together and have a rational discussion about what American election laws should be. They must be guided by the American people rather than blind adherence to ideology or the desires of small-but-powerful activist groups.

To get to the election system that is best for Americans and our system of government (in that order), we need to establish a simple, accepted goal: every American citizen who is eligible to vote should be able to do so securely and easily and have his or her vote counted—exactly once. Every election rule we make must be in pursuit of this goal and no other. Focusing on this single imperative makes developing commonsense, bipartisan election laws much simpler.

VOTER IDENTIFICATION

The most basic requirement for meeting our stated rule—and enabling all the following standards for a fair election—is being able to make sure we know who is voting. Voter ID laws allow election officials to quickly ensure that people are who they say they are, that they are eligible to vote, and that they only vote once. As I mentioned in a previous chapter, Speaker Pelosi's "Corrupt Politicians Act" sought to override or undermine voter identification requirements in many states by dictating that a signed affidavit or the last four digits of one's Social Security number could serve as identification. Of course, it is likely that someone who is willing to commit election fraud by casting an illegal vote is also willing to lie on a sheet of paper. Further, hearing four numbers from a person does nothing to help an election official immediately determine a voter's eligibility to cast a ballot.

What is simpler than relying on government-issued photo identification to help secure elections? The American Civil Liberties Union (ACLU)—which has sued numerous states to stop voter identification laws—claims that voter ID laws discriminate against elderly and minority Americans, saying that many people in poorer, minority communities do not have photo ID. Citing a 2006 telephone survey of 987 people sponsored by the Brennan Center for Justice at NYU School of Law, the ACLU reports that as many as 11 percent of U.S. citizens do not have government-issued photo identification. Using now-21-year-old census data, the survey extrapolates this figure out to 21 million potential Americans.[2] The ACLU argues that it is too expensive and too difficult for many of these Americans to access the documents needed to secure a government-issued photo ID.

Now, even if this extrapolation of a telephone survey of fewer than 1,000 people was an accurate representation of the country, it was accurate in 2006. According to Pew Research, only 71 percent of American adults had access to the internet in 2006. Now 93 percent of adults say they use the internet.[3] It is now far easier and less costly to gain the necessary documents and get a photo ID. Further, many states specifically provide photo identification cards for voting—free of charge. It is time we stop the nonsense. If you fly on any domestic or international flight, you need a photo ID to get on the plane. If you want to buy alcohol or tobacco products anywhere in the United States, you must show government-issued photo ID. Voting is more important than going to Las Vegas or drinking a beer. Voting should require a photo ID, too.

Finally, the best argument for photo identification requirements for voting is that there is a vast American majority who wants it. A 2021 McLaughlin & Associates nationwide survey found that 78 percent of Americans are for "voter ID requirements in elections which requires voters to present a valid, government issued form of identification to prove they are who they say they are, when casting their vote or requesting an absentee ballot."

According to the survey company:

"Only 17% opposed. 92% of Trump voters and 66% of Biden voters support this measure. Strong majority support for voter ID for ballots including absentee ballots extends across all partisan, ideological and demographic voter segments including 83% among whites, 72% among African Americans and 61% among Hispanics."

And the McLaughlin poll is not the only one. In 2018, Pew Research found that 76 percent of Americans "favored requiring all voters to show government-issued photo identification to vote. The vast majority of Republicans (91%) backed ID requirements, while a smaller majority of Democrats (63%) said the same."[4]

Establishing photo ID requirements for all voting fixes most of the biggest concerns about election integrity. Importantly, it would be an enormous step toward restoring Americans' trust in our elections. Let's stop the partisan fighting and just do it.

ACCURATE VOTER ROLLS

Part and parcel with photo ID requirements, we also must have accurate, complete voter registration lists if we are going to be able to ensure elections are secure and fair. The last major federal legislation that dealt with voter registration was the National Voter Registration Act of 1993. This greatly expanded voter registrations by requiring that states provide the option for voters to register to vote when they apply to obtain a driver's license. It also directed states to make voter registration materials available at all public buildings, provide the ability to register to vote by mail, and a slew of other provisions. It was an important legislative effort, but it was written in the mid-1990s.

As the Pew Trusts' Center on the States reported in 2012, "Voter registration in the United States largely reflects its 19th-century origins and has not kept pace with advancing technology and a mobile society. States' systems must be brought into the 21st century to be more accurate, cost-effective, and efficient."

The main finding of the Pew Trusts report was that America's voter registration systems "are plagued with errors and inefficiencies that waste taxpayer dollars, undermine voter confidence, and fuel partisan disputes over the integrity of our elections."[5]

This was in 2012—nearly ten years ago—and nothing significant has been done at the federal level to fix these problems. Instead, congressional Democrats are pushing efforts to automatically add people to voter lists virtually anytime they interact with a public institution (including public high schools and universities). So called Automatic Voter Registration is billed as a way to make sure all eligible voters in a given state are registered. The problem is it creates massive potential for names to be duplicated and for ineligible voters to be registered without their knowledge or intent.

Even the American Bar Association, which has become incredibly left-leaning in recent decades, says this effort is bad policy. Immigrants who are seeking to become naturalized as legal citizens who are automatically added to voter rolls by states could suddenly find their legal immigration status jeopardized. According to the ABA:[6]

"Whether a non-citizen national with a passport or one who is accidentally added due to clerical mistakes by government officials, non-citizens erroneously registered through AVR can face serious immigration consequences, such as deportation or becoming ineligible to naturalize. Under immigration law, making a false claim to U.S. citizenship is a federal felony regardless of knowledge or intent. Additionally, non-citizens are prohibited from voting in federal elections, where liability is triggered if a person does the targeted act consciously, regardless of intent or understanding of the illegality of the act."

If such a system is pursued, the ABA says there should be a proactive opt-out provision where the person being registered can stop the process. In the end, this is only slightly different from what current law already provides. Why tie up Congress for potentially two years on an effort that moves the ball one partisan inch?

Congressional Democrats are also trying to make it harder for state election officials to remove the names of people who should not be on the list (people who moved, died, are not U.S. citizens, or were convicted of felonies). By effectively preventing state officials from performing standard list maintenance that is required by federal law, these efforts could sew even more mistrust and skepticism about our elections. They would also make it harder to have fair, accurate elections. As the National Association of State Legislators explains:

> "The goal of maintaining an accurate voter list is to ensure that eligible voters are able to cast a ballot, to keep track of who has voted to prevent anyone from voting twice and, by reducing inaccuracies, speed up the voter check-in process at polling places. *Voter registration lists are the foundation of everything else in election administration*"[7] (emphasis mine).

We already know that many of our voter lists need serious cleaning. The 2012 Pew Trusts study found that 24 million voter registrations nationwide were invalid or "significantly inaccurate." That's one-eighth of all the registrations. Pew found more than 1.8 million registered voters were deceased and roughly 2.75 million people were registered in multiple states.[8]

Regular list maintenance has been a part of state election officials' duties for decades, but it has recently become a favorite topic of radical, left-wing activists, who like to refer to the legal process of cleaning voter rolls as "purging." They claim that Republican election officials are only trying to clean the lists to disenfranchise minority voters who sometimes are removed from voter rolls in the process. At the same time, the legal watchdog Judicial Watch had to sue the state of California for refusing to keep accurate voter lists. The state ultimately settled in 2019 and agreed to remove as many as 1.5 million inactive names from its voter rolls.[9]

This has been a big political fight for both the left and right in America in recent years, but it is—at its core—a stupid one to have. We want accurate voter lists, so we need to regularly remove the names of people who have moved, died, or otherwise become ineligible to vote. But we also want to ensure every eligible voter can vote. There's a simple solution: let people register whenever they cast their ballots, so long as they show a government-issued photo ID that proves who they are and where they live.

It really can be this simple.

ABSENTEE BALLOTS

The absentee ballot fight is another one that could be avoided if we have both photo ID requirements and accurate voter lists. Essentially, states could switch to all absentee ballots if election officials had a way to instantly verify the identity of the person who filled out the ballot, their eligibility to vote, and that he or she had only voted once.

One way to do this would be simply to require that voters provide a copy of their photo ID with their mailed-in ballot material (remember, 81 percent of Americans support photo IDs for voting). This could be in addition to signature verification (which McLaughlin & Associates found 85 percent of Americans support for mail-in ballots). With these two simple provisions, election officials could immediately check the person's name, signature, and address against accurate, up-to-date voter registration records to verify the ballot is valid. If there were discrepancies, the ballot could be marked provisional, and the person could be contacted to provide more information.

Further, states should develop secure online databases that residents could use to look up their votes (and only their votes) to see if and how they were counted. This would add another layer of accountability to our elections and alleviate skepticism. To be clear, I do not want this to be a federal database—or for the federal government to claw any authority from states to run elections. Instead, the federal government could provide revenue-neutral block grants or other funding mechanisms to support these kinds of election integrity measures.

However, the only way a robust, honest mail-in voting system can work is if the chain of custody for ballots is ironclad. There cannot be widespread third-party ballot collection—or ballot harvesting. Now, I don't have a problem with third-party ballot collection so long as there are reasonable restrictions. Nearly a dozen states allow people to return ballots on behalf of their family members. Twenty-six states allow for voters to designate someone else regardless of relation to deliver their ballot. In those cases, the ballot envelopes need to be signed and witnessed. In theory, this system could work if the chain of custody for the ballot is clear and the designated person delivering the ballot provides photo ID and takes legal responsibility for seeing that the ballot is delivered. There must also be tight limits on how many ballots per election a single ballot carrier can deliver.

However, without restrictions, this practice can become seriously coercive and degrade our election integrity. In states such as California and Nevada, where there are no limits to how many ballots a single ballot collector could turn in, a single person could suddenly be able to sway the results of an election (by either destroying or selectively delivering ballots).

In most cases, ballot collectors are either volunteers or staff members of a local party or political organization. In an unfettered ballot harvesting regime, there would be nothing material stopping a ballot collector from coercing, threatening, or bribing people to fill out their absentee ballots for a specific candidate. Think of all the many laws that states have against a party's trying to persuade voters at physical voting locations. In a situation where a party-paid ballot collector has a captive audience (such as at a nursing home), he or she could freely attempt to influence voters while they are filling out their ballots.

This brings up the second serious problem with mass ballot harvesting: the integrity of ballot secrecy. As Heritage Foundation senior legal fellow Hans A. von Spakovsky wrote on October 30, 2019:

"Allowing individuals other than the voter or his immediate family to handle absentee ballots is a recipe for mischief and wrongdoing. Neither voters nor election officials can verify that the secrecy of the ballot was not compromised or that the ballot submitted in the voter's name by a third party accurately reflects the voter's choices and was not fraudulently changed by the vote harvester. And there is no guarantee that vote harvesters won't simply discard the ballots of voters whose political preferences for candidates of the opposition party are known."[10]

Ballot secrecy is integral to modern American democracy. Any historian will note that it came about specifically because wealthy landlords, business owners, and other elites in power in the mid-1800s would threaten and punish their employees or renters who didn't vote as prescribed. As James D'Angelo and Brent Ranalli wrote for *Congressional Research*, the imposition of ballot security "brought an immediate reduction to election violence, intimidation and bribery. It also curtailed the Robber Barons' vise-grip control over elections and diminished their hold on the democratic process."[11]

An expansion of absentee voting could do wonders for people in rural areas, people who cannot easily vote in person, or people who are simply busy. While many factors played into the robust turnout of the 2020 election, expanded absentee voting certainly provided a serious boost. This is fine. I don't have a problem with voting being convenient. Again, we want every eligible person to vote securely—exactly once. However, if we want our elections to be secure—and for the American people to believe they are secure—we must have equally robust systems to ensure that absentee ballots are unaltered, uncoerced, and remain secret.

ENDING BIG TECH INFLUENCE

Of course, even if we have the best, most accurate, and most transparent voting system, we will not fully restore faith in our elections until we—as a society—can overcome the influence and power that social media companies and other Big Tech engines are beginning to impose upon our society.

To be perfectly clear: I am for free speech. I am not for the federal government dictating to social media companies what content they can and can't display on their properties. However, I no longer see value in affording social media companies the special protections they have over being responsible for lies, libel, and defamation that are promoted on their platforms. At this point, Twitter, Facebook, and others have clearly displayed that they have the capability—and indeed established systems—to monitor and exercise editorial control over content posted on their platforms. (I was banned from Twitter in early 2021 for a little more than a week over a tweet about concerns that people illegally crossing the southern border were not being tested for COVID-19.)

It seems clear to me that Section 230 of the Communications Decency Act is no longer necessary. *The New York Times, The Washington Post*, CNN or any other traditional media company is responsible for the things its own staff and outside commenters post on its platforms. At the time when social media was new, Congress created Section 230 to allow these new communications platforms to operate free of the fear of massive lawsuits. It is abundantly clear now that the Big Tech giants have the technology to take responsibility for their content and no longer require special treatment from the government.

We must recognize that the biggest social media companies are more like Russian oligarchs than typical American media organizations. We must develop a new generation of solutions to meet the challenges and threats posed by these enormous concentrations of money, power, and ego.

This, by itself, should help make social media platforms much more honest and selective about censoring the American people.

CHAPTER SIX

UNDERSTANDING AND DEFEATING WOKEISM

T he biggest cultural fight happening right now is between free speech, civil discourse, and wokeism.

One of the most difficult things about understanding and fighting wokeism is that it uses a virtually incomprehensible vocabulary. Its devotees use new words and phrases concocted in university faculty lounges, and they also redefine words to mean something different. Sometimes the redefined words mean the total opposite of what they meant before. This is done deliberately to obscure the radical and totalitarian nature of this movement behind pleasant and noble-sounding rhetoric.

In fact, wokeism is a toxic stew of left-wing philosophies that have merged into a self-perpetuating eruption of destructive nonsense flowing down from our universities into our K–12 classrooms, corporate boardrooms, and government centers. If you want an example of the simultaneously confusing, comical, and deeply dangerous nature of the woke movement—and how it is infecting every institution in our society—take a look at a recruitment video put out by the Central Intelligence Agency in March 2021. The video follows an agent around CIA headquarters in Langley, Virginia, as she engages in a long, jargon-laden monologue of self-satisfied navel gazing. It features lines such as:

- "Nothing about me was or is tragic. I am perfectly made."
- "I'm a woman of color. I am a mom. I am a cisgender millennial who has been diagnosed with generalized anxiety disorder."
- "I am intersectional. But my existence is not a box checking exercise. I am a walking declaration, a woman whose inflection does not rise at the end of her sentences, suggesting that a question has been asked."
- "I used to struggle with imposter syndrome. But at 36 I refuse to internalize misguided patriarchal ideas of what a woman can or should be. I am tired of feeling like I'm supposed to apologize for the space I occupy rather than intoxicate people with my effort . . . my brilliance. I am proud of me. Full stop."
- "I am unapologetically me. I want you to be unapologetically you, whoever you are. Know your worth and command your space. Mija you're worth it."

America's enemies must really be shaking in their boots.

Can you imagine Tom Brokaw's Greatest Generation defeating the German Nazis, Italian Fascists, and Japanese imperial military with this kind of touchy-feely, inward-looking focus on meeism?

How is it possible that the CIA—the institution dedicated to the vital task of protecting our nation's secrets (and stealing those of our enemies)—got hijacked to become a purveyor of a radical left-wing ideology?

In this chapter, I will attempt to translate the woke movement's vocabulary into plain English and give you a broad overview of why its underlying assumptions are at odds with fundamental American values and the basic principles of liberal democracy. We will also explain how it has grown to infect every major institution in our society and discuss ways to fight back.

CLASS CONSCIOUSNESS AND THE CRITICAL THEORY VIRUS

Being "woke" is a new term, but it is an old idea.

Karl Marx, the father of communism, and his Marxist disciples wrote about achieving "class consciousness"—a state of being in which a person finally understands that the working class are oppressed by the owners of production and property and commits themselves to revolution to overthrow their bosses. Marxists believe that when enough people have achieved class consciousness, revolution can happen that will eventually lead the way to a communist utopia.

False consciousness, in contrast, is how Marxists view any other conception of how a person thinks of themselves and society due to accepting the ideology, religion, or narratives of the ruling class. In other words, until you recognize your oppression (or your role in oppressing others) and commit to revolution, you are asleep. When you achieve class consciousness, you are finally awake. Or woke.

The only meaningful difference between the radical left's class consciousness of a hundred years ago and the radical left's wokeness of today is in how they are choosing to divide people. Before it was economic status. Now it is by fixed identity traits, such as race, gender, and sexuality. (In fact, being woke is sometimes explicitly referred to as achieving racial consciousness.)

This view of the world as being singularly defined by power and oppression comes from a school of academic thought called critical theory. Critical theory is a virus. This is not my description; it is the analogy of two feminist scholars who approvingly describe the point of women's studies to send forth infectious agents into other fields to disrupt them.[1]

The virus metaphor explains why after gaining a foothold in university literature departments as a way to interpret *fiction*, critical theory rapidly expanded into countless other disciplines that are supposed to help us understand *reality*. The one you hear discussed the most is Critical Race Theory, but there is also Critical Legal Theory, Critical Pedagogy (teaching), Critical Social Justice, Critical Sociology, and even Critical Math and Science. From these strongholds in academia, critical theory is now sending super spreaders into all our major institutions.

As I am writing this, we are nearing the end of the COVID-19 pandemic. We are at the beginning of the critical theory pandemic, and signs of infection are everywhere. Major corporations such as Disney and Coca-Cola are mandating their employees take racial sensitivity training based on Critical Race Theory, where they learn that white people are inherently racist and cannot help playing a role in oppressing people of color.[2,3] For years, conservatives made fun of liberals taking useless classes in university. Turns out the joke was on us. All these brainwashed students became human resources managers and got into other c-suite positions that were able to coerce industry into becoming another vehicle for woke ideology.

Public school systems are adopting critical theory principles into their curriculums. This would be bad enough if it were just limited to subjects such as history, but it is also infecting math and science education. How can math be racist, you might ask? Apparently, you are unaware that insisting that students produce the right answer is a manifestation of white supremacy. You monster. Teachers that object to the new regime are being told to resign and find jobs elsewhere.[4]

The American Medical Association recently announced a strategic plan to "embed racial justice" into the medical profession.[5] What might that look like? We got a good preview in the early days of the COVID-19 vaccine rollout. Some states kept it simple. They tried to get as many shots in people's arms as possible, as fast as possible. They did well. Others created highly complicated priority tiers, including racial preferences, which slowed down distribution and led to waste.[6] Still, despite this failure, two doctors recently made the case that the COVID-19 experience shows why we need to end colorblind policies in medicine and prioritize access based on race to address historical inequities.[7]

Our institutions of national security are also infected. I already mentioned the woke CIA ad. There is a similar series of ads for the U.S. Army. And a senior officer in the Space Force was recently fired for speaking out against Critical Race Theory being taught in the military.[8]

Wokeism hijacks institutions and turns them into vehicles for more wokeism. Once you've given power to ideologues in your organization, their goal is not to help it achieve its primary mission. Their goal is to reorient it into an engine for revolution.

THE TRUTH DOESN'T MATTER

Let me be as blunt as possible: critical theory is a dangerous, cynical lie.

The big lie of critical theory is that on a planet of 6 billion people with ten thousand years of civilization, millions of years of evolution, and a near infinite number of influences ranging from history, to biology, to the environment, and more, that any truth can be discovered by interpreting reality through the single, narrow lens of power and oppression. The cynicism comes from the fact that the proponents of critical theory understand this, but don't care. That's because arriving at the truth is explicitly not the point of critical theory. The point is revolution.

Critical theory draws from many left-wing schools of thought, but the most influential (aside from Marxism) is postmodernism. This connection to postmodernism is important to understand because it explains why at its philosophical core, wokeism is at odds with the basic values and tenets of liberal democracy. Postmodernism is a rejection of the Enlightenment principles that inspired the American Revolution, our system of government, classical liberalism, and the spread of freedom and free markets throughout the globe.

Don't take my word for it. One of the authoritative textbooks on Critical Race Theory defines it explicitly as an anti-liberal (in the classical meaning of the word), anti-Enlightenment, and anti-constitutional discipline:

"Unlike traditional civil rights discourse, which stresses incrementalism and step-by-step progress, critical race theory questions the very foundations of the liberal order, including equality theory, legal reasoning, Enlightenment rationalism, and neutral principles of constitutional law."[9]

I recently had Douglas Murray on my podcast, *Newt's World*, to discuss his book *The Madness of Crowds: Gender, Race, and Identity*. His description of critical theory—and the woke movement it has inspired—is similar to that of a virus. He calls it "societal malware." Malware is software that is specifically designed to disrupt, damage, or gain unauthorized access to a computer system. It is a specific type of computer virus. Critical theory is malware for a society built upon the tenets of the Enlightenment.

Enlightenment principles are based on the idea of an objective truth that can be discovered through methodical, rational inquiry. Importantly, enlightenment thinking acknowledges that human beings have biases, and builds checks and balances into its systems to compensate. This basic framework of checks and balances can be seen in the constitutions of Western democracies such as the United States. But it is also seen in the rigorous approach of the scientific method, which requires scientists to prove their theories true by falsifying the alternatives and the use of peer review.

By contrast, postmodernists believe our ability to observe the world is so distorted by social circumstances that the truth is unknowable. Therefore, they view science and reason as tools of oppression since they are captured by those with power. This is why the woke will often talk about the importance of "lived experience" rather than hard data when it comes to understanding the impact of racism and sexism. "You are denying my lived experience!" is a common refrain from the woke, and it is used to shut down debate rather than enhance it.

So critical theory is not a search for the truth, since the woke don't believe in truth. Instead, critical theory is explicitly activist in nature. One of the intellectual founders described the goal of critical theory as "to liberate human beings from the circumstances that enslave them."[10] The goal of critical theory is to deconstruct our understanding of reality into a narrative of oppressor and oppressed to further the revolution. Whether that interpretation of reality is true is beside the point.

CANCEL CULTURE VS. FREE SPEECH

The woke movement's anti-liberal foundation and disdain for objective truth give us the proper framework to understand the cancel culture of the left.

Freedom of speech is not just a legal protection from government censorship; it is also a value. A society that values freedom of speech encourages the free and respectful exchange of ideas. It believes that the answer to bad speech is good speech. The answer to bad ideas is good ideas. This how you keep truly dangerous ideas limited to a small minority while allowing for new ideas that have merit to get a fair hearing.

Cancel culture is a violation of this ethos. It suppresses any speech that is not politically correct as a brute exercise of power.

It is particularly ironic that the woke are such adamant practitioners of cancel culture because it inherently benefits those with the power to set the cultural agenda.

Cancel culture takes many forms.

It comes in the form of guest speakers and professors being driven off university campuses by mobs of woke protesters. Heather Mac Donald is a researcher and author who uses publicly available data to debunk the woke narrative of racist policing. She was supposed to speak at Claremont McKenna College in 2017 but the event was canceled at the last minute when more than two hundred protestors encircled the venue and refused to let anyone enter. The woke had no compunction about violating Mac Donald's freedom to speak her mind or an audience's right to listen. There are also several cases of professors (many of them liberals) being driven off campus after expressing opinions contrary to woke anti-liberal ideology.

It also comes in the form of online mobs that seize on people's comments—sometimes celebrities, sometimes ordinary citizens—to whip up a frenzy of outrage and calls for punishment to coerce people into apologizing. These online outrage mobs mirror the "struggle sessions" used in the Maoist cultural revolution in China, where critics of the new communist regime were paraded in front of their peers, or even large crowds, and verbally abused until they confessed.

The most insidious example of cancel culture is that practiced by the big tech companies, which are overwhelmingly dominated by the woke, both at the managerial and programmer level. Over the past several years, there have been several high-profile cases of social media posts being taken down or slapped with warning labels, most notably including the former president of the United States, Donald Trump. But even more dangerous is these companies' ability to hide content they don't want to appear in our social media feeds and search results. We have no idea what kind of censorship is occurring in the online world because the algorithms they are using to decide what gets featured and what gets buried are a trade secret.

The woke believe they can get away with this for a simple reason: they really do not believe in universal human rights, including freedom of speech.

This again is due to the woke ideology's foundation of postmodernism. It was Enlightenment thinking that was responsible for the development of the idea of individual rights that come from God or nature rather than the state. This is the American framework, articulated in the Declaration of Independence that humans are "endowed by their Creator with certain unalienable rights," and that while it is the responsibility of the government to secure those rights, government is not the source of them.

Critical theory's postmodern foundation rejects this view of human rights. To postmodernists, there is nothing universally true about human nature; it is all a social construct. This includes the notion of universal human rights. To postmodernists, individuals do not have rights, groups do. And the government is responsible for granting them, not protecting them. So, the postmodern foundation of wokeism rejects the idea that freedom of speech even exists.

Meanwhile, the critical theory interpretation of the world teaches that the construct of freedom of speech is a tool for perpetuating power imbalances, since those in power use it to perpetuate the false consciousness that is enslaving everyone else. The fact that this interpretation is false, and that protecting and cherishing freedom of speech is one of the greatest things we can do to equalize power, is, again, besides the point. The woke don't care about truth, only about the advancement of their narrative.

THE OPPRESSION OLYMPICS

Critical theory teaches the woke that there is a hierarchy of oppression in the world. At the top sit straight, white, "cisgender" (meaning their biological sex aligns with what gender they feel they are), Christian men. They have the most of what the woke call "privilege," and because of that, their opinions should be dismissed—unless, of course, they are apologizing for being born and parroting woke ideology, in which case they are being an "ally."

At the bottom of the ladder of oppression sit gay, transgender, disabled, black, female, refugee Druids. Probably. Maybe it is some other combination. It is hard to keep track of who is considered most oppressed by the woke. Their worldview treats identity characteristics like a form of social currency, and there is intense competition to be seen as the most oppressed. The more allegedly oppressed subgroups you identify with, the more your voice matters when it comes to issues of social justice. Unless, of course, you have an opinion heretical to woke ideology. Then it doesn't matter how many allegedly oppressed identity characteristics you possess. Anyone who expresses opinions that do not fit into the woke narrative is declared to have an inauthentic voice or having internalized oppression/racism—in other words, a false consciousness. Again, this is straight out of Marxism.

For a perfect example of these attacks, look at the response Tim Scott, an African American Republican senator from South Carolina, generated from the left when he delivered the Republican rebuttal to President Biden's first address to Congress in May 2021. In his response, he spoke out boldly against the dangerous woke worldview and racialized politics of the American left:

> "When America comes together, we've made tremendous progress. But powerful forces want to pull us apart. A hundred years ago, kids in classrooms were taught the color of their skin was their most important characteristic. And if they looked a certain way, they were inferior.
>
> "Today, kids again are being taught that the color of their skin defines them, and if they look a certain way, they're an oppressor. From colleges to corporations to our culture, people are making money and gaining power by pretending we haven't made any progress at all, by doubling down on the divisions we've worked so hard to heal.
>
> "You know this stuff is wrong. Hear me clearly: America is not a racist country. It's backwards to fight discrimination with different types of discrimination. And it's wrong to try to use our painful past to dishonestly shut down debates in the present."

Senator Scott's speech was powerful because he bluntly told the truth about Critical Race Theory and woke ideology—it is immoral and based on a lie. That's why the response from the left was so intense and vile.

Gary O'Connor, the chairman of the Lamar County Democratic Party in Texas, accused Scott of being an "oreo," a racial slur for a Black person who adopts white views (in other words, like the cookie, they're black on the outside but white on the inside). O'Connor later resigned.[11]

The social media company Twitter allowed "Uncle Tim"—a derivation on a racial slur—to trend on its site for twelve hours.[12] For a term to trend means that tens of thousands of people must have been using it. The website eventually blocked the term from appearing on its trending section but did not immediately delete the tweets or suspend the accounts of those using the term, despite it being hate speech and seemingly in violation of its terms of service.[13]

One of those people was former MSNBC host Touré Neblett, who tweeted, "Tim Scott gets called Uncle Tom by progressives. But he's an Uncle Tim."[14] The left-wing network was full of similarly grotesque commentary from their hosts. Nicole Wallace accused Scott of being a puppet, claiming that someone close to Trump must have helped write the speech, and Joy Reid said his speech was "standard Republican pablum" that could have been delivered by GOP senators Tom Cotton or Mike Lee (both white).[15, 16]

Meanwhile, left-wing, so-called representatives of the Black community were apoplectic.

Bishop Talbert Swan, a black pastor from Massachusetts, tweeted, "Uncle Tim has perfected the art of sycophantic bootlicking. He's a master step n fetch it artist and cunning white supremacy apologist, who demonstrated his buck dancing skills in front of the entire world." Swan was referring to Stepin Fetchit, the stage name of Lincoln Theodore Monroe Andrew Perry, who was the first Black actor to have a successful film career, but whose characters began to be criticized as being reinforcing negative stereotypes of Black people. In other words, Swan was accusing Scott of playing a character that appeals to white people but is harmful to Blacks.

Jesse Jackson also chimed in. He called Senator Scott's logic "sick" and claimed Republicans were manipulating him. He added that Republicans "try to make Clarence Thomas and Thurgood Marshall interchangeable."[17] In other words, Jackson is saying that Black conservatives don't count as authentic Black voices.

The message to other Black (or gay, immigrant, etc.) conservatives is clear: shut up or you will get pilloried, too.

REDEFINING RACISM

For some on the woke left, Senator Scott's speech was an opportunity to advance a key strategic objective for their movement: redefining racism.

Our common understanding of racism is actions, both individual and collective (such as laws), that treat members of one racial group differently than another. The problem for the woke is that ending discrimination is not a big enough target for their ambition. Remember, like communism, wokeism is a revolutionary movement that seeks to overthrow the existing society and engineer a new one using the brute force of government to redistribute wealth and power. The woke don't want to end discrimination; they want to discriminate based on their value system. That's why its leaders have started talking about "institutional" or "systemic racism."

For instance, Dr. Rayshawn Ray of the Brookings Institution argued that Senator Scott's claim that America was not racist was, in fact, a clear-cut example of systemic racism.[18] Joy Behar, cohost of ABC's *The View* and a white woman, took the opportunity to lecture Senator Scott about systemic racism. "Now, Tim Scott, he does not seem to understand . . . the difference between a racist country and systemic racism."[19]

As the woke movement defines it, systemic racism is something much broader than the unequal treatment of people of a certain race. The woke believe racism pervades all of society, affects all our institutions and policies, and manifests itself in every single interaction we have as a people. As a result of this mindset, the woke see racism everywhere and feel compelled to "call it out" so it can be dismantled. This process is referred to as "problematizing" and it can be illustrated with these recent headlines from left-wing media finding racism and sexism in everything.

- The Unbearable Whiteness of Hiking and How to Solve It (Sierra Club)[20]
- The Unbearable Whiteness of Baseball (*New York Times*)[21]
- How Star Wars Reinforces Our Prejudices (*Washington Post*)[22]
- The Racism of Technology—and Why Driverless Cars Could Be the Most Dangerous Example Yet (*Guardian*)[23]
- The Grocery Store Shows Us How Systemic Racism Works (Medium)[24]
- "Western Civilization" means Classics . . . and White Supremacy (Pharos)[25]
- Addressing Anti-Blackness in Specialty Coffee (Urnex)[26]
- Why Is American Classical Music So White? (NPR)[27]
- Systemic Racism Can't Be Fixed Without Tackling It Within Cycling (Bicycling)[28]

- Why Heterosexual Relationships Are So Bad for Us, According to a Sex Researcher (Insider)[29]
- The Candy Industry Has a Long History of Racism That We Can't Ignore (Spoon University)[30]

It is easy to laugh at the silliness of this mindset. After all, if you wear red-tinted sunglasses, you should not be surprised to see that everything has a pinkish hue. The woke are viewing everything through the narrow lens of critical theory, so they see racism, sexism, and other "isms" everywhere they look.

Of course, normal people don't see the world this way. Ibram X. Kendi is one of the most influential figures in the woke movement. He has bestselling books—including a children's book, *Anti-Racist Baby*—and has appeared on countless talk shows and given speeches all over the world explaining his ideology. But in his most famous book, *How to Be an Anti-Racist*, he makes a stunning admission:

> "I struggle to concretely explain what 'institutional racism' means to the Middle Eastern small businessman, the Black service worker, the White teacher, the Latinx nurse, the Asian factory worker, and the Native store clerk who do not take the courses on racism, do not read the books on racism, do not go to the lectures on racism, do not watch the specials on racism, do not listen to the podcasts on racism, do not attend the rallies against racism."

You would think the fact that the targets of institutional racism are skeptical of its existence should be a clue to the woke, but that would require thinking rationally—which isn't postmodern.

Besides, problematizing serves an important strategic value for wokeism and it relates once again back to Marxism and the concept of false consciousness. Marxist apologists believe that the reason why communism never took hold in the West was that the capitalists had a hegemonic control of the culture that preserved the false consciousness of the masses.

The woke left have internalized this lesson and are seeking to delegitimize everything in our culture that we value as part of an invisible web of oppression designed to subjugate people of color for the benefit of whites. And as the sample headlines show, they mark everything with the scarlet R of racism—from the trivial, like specialty coffee, to the foundations of Western civilization, like the "Classics." This serves a simple purpose: to delegitimize America and Western civilization to make us willing to throw it all away.

This is why the platforms and language of woke organizations that are supposedly focused on racial justice often include things that seem completely out of left field (pun intended). To them, it is all racist. Unsurprisingly, given that the founders of Black Lives Matter have described themselves as "trained Marxists," a common focus of their ire is capitalism. For instance, the Washington, D.C., chapter of the organization defines itself as "creating the conditions for Black Liberation through the abolition of systems and institutions of white supremacy, capitalism, patriarchy and colonialism."

Black Lives Matter and other similar organizations also routinely use language attacking the nuclear family. Until this section was scrubbed from its website, Black Lives Matter stated that one of its objectives was to "disrupt the Western-prescribed nuclear family structure requirement by supporting each other as extended families and 'villages' that collectively care for one another . . ."[31]

Nancy Pelosi and the Democratic machine are dutifully playing their part in this process of delegitimization, too. On their first day in the new Congress, the House passed a rule erasing "mother," "father," "son," "daughter," and more than two dozen gendered terms from the House rules document. Instead of "mother," they use the terms "birthing person" in congressional hearings and in floor speeches. The Biden budget request for 2022 included more than $200 million in spending for reducing "the high rate of maternal mortality and race-based disparities in outcomes among birthing people."[32]

There is no more important foundational institution in our society than that of the family. It is where we adopt most of our values and learn most of our assumptions about the world. The woke left would rather we get those values from their university professors, K–12 curriculum, and certified diversity trainers. That's why the woke left want to delegitimize the family—so we are more willing to throw away the values passed on through generations in favor of a radical new experiment.

SELECTIVE RACISM

At the same time the woke are expanding the definition of racism into an amorphous blog that infects every aspect of our society, they add an asterisk to its definition. The woke redefine racism so that it can only occur when it is perpetrated by or occurs for the benefit of identity groups that are higher on their hierarchy of power and privilege.

Robin D'Angelo is an author, speaker consultant, and professor of education whose work is frequently pushed as must reading by the woke movement. She is the most famous figure in the booming field of "whiteness studies" (yes, this is a real thing). Her most famous work is *White Fragility: Why It's So Hard for White People to Talk About Racism* and she has developed a curriculum that is often licensed by large corporations and other institutions that is supposed to teach white people how to be less racist.

In *Is Everyone Really Equal? An Introduction to Key Concepts in Social Justice Education,* she defines racism in this way:

"From a critical social justice perspective, the term racism refers to this system of collective social and institutional White power and privilege.

"Racism: White racial and cultural prejudice and discrimination, supported by institutional power and authority, used to the advantage of Whites and the disadvantage of people of Color. Racism encompasses economic, political, social, and institutional actions and beliefs that systematize and perpetuate an unequal distribution of privileges, resources, and power between Whites and people of Color."

The idea of "whiteness" is a key concept for the woke and they want white people to become hyperaware of their racial identity. They argue that a key characteristic of whiteness is being oblivious to the impact of racism, which makes them complicit in white supremacy, and it is only by obsessing over how being white gives them unearned privilege that a white person can be less complicit.

Here are some more passages from D'Angelo's work:

■ "The question is not 'did racism take place?' but rather, 'how did racism manifest in this situation?'"[33]

■ "STOP: Remember that it isn't actually possible to see everyone as an individual and thus to treat them as one. From a critical social justice perspective we understand that we are all socialized to see people from groups other than our own in particular and often problematic ways."[34]

It is remarkable how the woke have abandoned the goal of colorblindness in favor of hyperawareness of race. Certainly, we should recognize that our brains are hardwired to make snap judgments, so we need to be aware of that tendency and make a conscious effort to treat people fairly. In other words, while colorblindness may not be possible in a literal sense, it is absolutely an ideal we should strive for in our actions. But wokeism rejects the idea that this is possible, or even a goal worth pursuing. This is another profound break from the ideals of the Declaration of Independence and the civil rights movement of the 1960s that appealed to them to make the case for ending segregation.

Here is more D'Angelo:

■ "A positive white identity is an impossible goal. White identity is inherently racist; white people do not exist outside the system of white supremacy."[35]
■ "I strive to be 'less white.' To be less white is to: be less oppressive, less arrogant, less certain, less defensive, less ignorant, more humble."

Imagine for a second replacing the word "white" with "black" in either of those last two sentences and it is clear how racist they are.

It actually gets much worse.

The Yale School of Medicine's Department of Child Study Center hosted a lecture in April 2021 titled "The Psychopathic Problem of the White Mind." The speaker, Dr. Aruna Khilanani, remarked during her lecture, "White people are out of their minds and have been for a long time," and bragged about cutting most white people out of her life. She also adds, "I had fantasies about unloading a revolver into the head of any white person that got in my way, burying their body, and wiping bloody hands as I walked away relatively guiltless with a bounce in my step. Like I did the world a[n expletive] favor."[36]

Again, this goes back to the Marxist concept of false consciousness. The woke believe that most white people suffer from false consciousness of not identifying as an oppressor. So radical steps need to be taken to wake them up.

The aforementioned Ibram X. Kendi states explicitly that schools should be used as centers of indoctrination rather than education: "I had to forsake the suasionist bred into me, of researching and educating for the sake of changing minds." He continues, "Educational and moral suasion is not only a failed . . . [and] . . . suicidal strategy" and argues that teachers must "literally teach their students anti-racist ideas," otherwise they "effectively allow their students to be educated to be racist."

This is an argument for brainwashing and indoctrination over education.

Here is Kate Slater, an "anti-racist scholar" at the University of New Hampshire: "I am white. White people can never be anything but oppressors. . . . Being complicit with racism is something that we as white people just are. . . . I will work on my anti-racism my whole life but will continually fail. I will never get to a space where I am good enough."

This is not the language of a rational argument; it is more of a prayer. The woke define whiteness in purely negative terms and then force white people to identify with that negativity. This is cultlike behavior, targeting people's self-esteem and sense of personal identity as the first step in brainwashing. And the woke are targeting your children as their next recruits.

THE WOKE WAR ON MERIT

For the woke, whiteness is not just a characteristic of power, it is an entire set of cultural patterns. They argue that most of what we think of as "normal" or the right way to do things in America is part of white culture, and that to expect or insist that others abide by those same principles is reinforcing white supremacy. And President Biden's Department of Education has made it clear they are dedicated to perpetuating this falsehood.

The Biden administration has proposed a "culturally responsive teaching and learning" of civics and American history. The executive order includes many of the woke buzzwords and holds up *The New York Times'* anti-American 1619 Project—that prominent historians have criticized as nonsense—as an example of the type of curriculum that students should absorb.[37] The goal of the Biden administration's initiative is to reorient civics education away from traditional American values because they are too associated with whiteness.

It is hard to overstate what a fundamental break this is from the traditional American framework. The classical American model is that there is a certain core set of ideas and values that are universally true. They are articulately spelled out in our Declaration of Independence—that all men are created equal and have unalienable rights endowed by their Creator—but also include the importance of the work ethic, entrepreneurship, and religious faith. The ideal vision of America is to be a beacon for all who believed in those values and were willing to live by them.

The civil rights movement of the 1960s succeeded because it appealed to this framework. It called on America to live up to its founding ideals by ending discriminatory laws and allowing Black Americans to be fully a part of American society.

This is not what wokeism is trying to do. Wokeism claims that American ideals are a lie. They are saying we need to abandon our common framework, because to insist that there is a normative American set of values only serves to further white supremacy.

Don't believe me? Look at these series of qualities that the Smithsonian African American Museum listed as "aspects and assumptions of white culture in the United States" on its "talking about race" section of its website: rugged individualism, nuclear family structure, emphasis on the scientific method, a Western-focused history, Protestant work ethic, future orientation, following schedules. The poster was eventually removed from its website after the controversy but the page on "whiteness" is still up.[38]

Imagine for a second being a young African American child with an interest in science, who learns from the African American Museum that his passion for chemistry or physics is the result of him selling out to white values. It also is hard to think of a more racist idea that hard work, punctuality, and future orientation are part of white culture, and that it is unreasonable to expect people of color to display these traits, but that is exactly what the woke imply with their arguments.[39]

One of my favorite institutions is the KIPP charter school systems. For years they succeeded in teaching poor, minority students where the unionized public school systems failed. They succeeded by raising standards and expectations of the students and the parents, not lowering them. But unfortunately, wokeism has infected this once fine institution as well. Last year, KIPP announced that it was abandoning its longtime slogan, "Work Hard, Be Nice." Why? Listen to this gibberish: "The slogan passively supports ongoing efforts to pacify and control Black and Brown bodies in order to better condition them to be compliant and further reproduce current social norms that center whiteness and meritocracy as normal."[40]

The war on hard work and merit is pervasive throughout education.

California's Department of Education has proposed a so-called anti-racist math framework that would stop grouping students according to ability level, essentially ending gifted and talented programs in the state.[41] Meanwhile, anti-racist educators want to group students by race, which they call "affinity grouping."[42] In other words, to be anti-racist, they advocate segregation.

The Denver public school system trains their teachers to learn the distinct characteristics of "white culture," like "there is such a thing as being objective," "being polite," and distinguishing between good and bad and right and wrong.[43]

The Oregon Department of Education has encouraged teachers to be trained in something called "ethnomathematics" in order to eliminate "white supremacy" from math curricula.[44] What are examples of this white supremacy? They cite practices such as requiring students to show their work and emphasize "getting the 'right answer.'"

Meanwhile, some anti-racist educators argue that requiring students to demonstrate subject matter expertise to get an A is racist because the idea of what a student should and should not know is a social construct. In this framework, a bad grade is evidence of a teacher's inability due to racism to recognize a student's knowledge rather than evidence of a student not having mastery of the course work.

This is the sort of lame excuse a wisecracking student might make for why he failed a test. It is alarming to see it embraced by supposed educators. That's because they are no longer educators; they are indoctrinators.

EQUITY OVER EQUALITY

The woke's power-dependent definition of racism also legitimizes its race-based public policy agenda of reparations and anti-white discrimination.

For the woke, it is not enough to be "not racist" (in other words, treat everyone equally). According to the woke, it is impossible to not be racist since racism is baked into everything. More important, the woke believe that treating everyone equally is a tactic used by those in power to retain their power, because if you treat people today who look like those who were oppressed in the past the same as those who look like those who were historically the oppressors, the impact of that historic oppression on people today will never be corrected.

Instead, you must be "anti-racist," which is a phrase coined by, again, Ibram X. Kendi. In *How to Be an Antiracist*, he explicitly endorses race-based discrimination as a key component of anti-racism: "The only remedy to past discrimination is present discrimination. The only remedy to present discrimination is future discrimination."

Or as Dena Simmons, founder of LiberatED, said to a room full of Naperville Community School District teachers in a seminar that was mandatory to attend, "If you are not an 'anti-racist' you are a racist, even if you are treating people with respect."

Anti-racists must commit themselves to dismantling institutional racism to achieve what they call racial equity. Equity is quite distinct than equality and is best understood as treating individuals unequally based on their race to achieve equal racial group outcomes. In other words, equality is about treating individuals the same no matter their group identity. Equity is about treating individuals differently based on their group identity to achieve equal group outcomes.

Democratic politicians who have generally shied away from explicitly embracing reparations and race-based discrimination because they understand it is unpopular with Americans have embraced the use of the term "equity" as a way of hiding their true intentions behind a nice-sounding word.

Just days before the election, then-senator Kamala Harris warned America that the Biden administration was going to go all in on race-based public policies, with a tweet sharing a video explaining the difference between equality and equity. "Equitable treatment means we all end up in the same place," the video says.[45] (Fact check: half true. Most of us will end up equal—equally poor and impoverished. The governing elite will remain quite comfortable.)

And sure enough, on his first day in office, President Joe Biden signed an executive order on advancing racial equity in the federal government.[46] The language of the order tries to hide its intentions behind language about impartiality, but it is clear that the policy is to create a shadow system of race-based hiring and distribution of resources. So, understand that when Democratic politicians use the word "equity," they are explicitly endorsing race-based government policies that actively discriminate.

CHAPTER SEVEN

THE MORAL CASE
AGAINST WOKEISM

There is no doubt that more work needs to be done to eliminate the impact that slavery and segregation still have today on Black Americans. There are also too many Americans who, because of their race, religion, or some immutable characteristics, are unfairly denied opportunities. This needs to change.

But woke ideology hijacks people's sympathy and desire to help into supporting a fundamentally immoral and dangerous ideology. At its core, wokeism is incompatible with the pursuit of civil rights and equality under the law—and with the way we treat our fellow citizens personally. This ideology must be understood, exposed, and defeated if America is to survive as a bastion of freedom and prosperity—and if progress is going to continue to be made in allowing Americans of all backgrounds the opportunity to achieve the American dream.

The most important step in fighting wokeism is choosing the grounds upon which the battle must be fought.

The purpose of explaining the philosophical foundation of wokeism in the previous chapter was to show why it is fundamentally wrong and immoral. This was done deliberately because we cannot stop wokeism by making a public policy argument. Public policy is secondary. Wokeism's appeal is that it has wrapped itself in a moral cause, so we can only stop wokeism by showing that it is immoral. This is how Ronald Reagan, Margaret Thatcher, and Pope John Paul II fought communism—on moral grounds. It was not an economic argument. It was one about freedom and fairness and what was right.

We must fight wokeness by showing it is immoral. And it is.

Wokeism judges people by the color of their skin, not by the content of their character.

Wokeism believes people today should be held responsible for what other people did in the past.

Wokeism robs people of their individuality, forcing them into groups.

Wokeism doesn't believe in individual rights, only group rights.

Wokeism rejects equal protection under the law in favor of discrimination based on skin color.

Wokeism rejects basic freedom of speech in favor of censorship and fear of the mob.

Wokeism rejects education in favor of indoctrination.

Wokeism rejects the notion of truth.

Wokeism doesn't believe that hard work and merit should be rewarded.

Wokeism divides us along racial and other lines rather than unifying us around a common American identity.

We must make this moral case. Despite the constant propaganda from the left, there is still broad patriotic sentiment with most of the American people and a profound agreement on core American values. Remember, McLaughlin & Associates found 87 percent of Americans see themselves primarily as Americans. Only 8 percent see themselves primarily as people of color. This majority includes 66 percent of African Americans and 76 percent of Hispanics.

Strong majorities of all ethnicities also agree that America is the greatest and freest country on earth. And a whopping 91 percent of Americans agree with Rev. Martin Luther King Jr. that the content of a person's character is more important than the color of his or her skin.

A Gallup/Knight Foundation poll in 2018 found that 61 percent of college students felt their campus climate prevents people from freely expressing themselves.[1] A full 70 percent of students preferred free, open speech to censorship of "offensive" or "biased" speech (although this was down from 78 percent the previous year).

We are already seeing the anti-woke backlash starting in the United Kingdom and other parts of Europe. It is only a matter of time before American institutions begin to see the same. Any American who values freedom of speech, freedom to practice religion, equal treatment under the law, and the belief that our skin color does not define us should be deeply concerned. Further, any American who wants to live in a country that is friendly, courteous, open-minded, and unified must work against the hateful, divisive, close-minded doctrine of wokeism and the cancel culture.

Wokeism violates all of America's founding values and is thus enormously vulnerable if we can reveal its true nature. There are several battlegrounds on which the woke ideology must be fought. In each of them, our message must be about right and wrong. We must appeal to the heart, not just the head.

EDUCATION OVER INDOCTRINATION

As author James A. Lindsey has observed, the threat posed by Critical Race Theory is not that it is being *taught* in schools; it is that it is being put into *practice*.[2] Radical school boards and teachers are mutating more and more of the classroom experience to comport with critical theory ideology.

We must fight back against the implementation of critical theory in our schools. Teachers and professors are free to sprout crazy left-wing ideas on their own time, but not in the classroom. There is something fundamentally insane about a society being forced to fund an ideology that teaches you to hate it. It is a pathway for America to devour itself. We should unapologetically demand that public dollars stop being used to indoctrinate Americans, especially children, in anti-American, racist ideology.

A growing number of states, including Idaho and Texas, have passed bills preventing tenets derived from Critical Race Theory from being taught using public dollars.[3] This includes K–12 schools, universities, and employee education for government workers. These are important steps and similar legislation should be introduced in every state in the union.

Woke apologists claim that these laws preventing indoctrination into Critical Race Theory in schools are attempts to whitewash American history, but this is a lie. There is nothing in these laws that prevents the facts of American history from being taught. This includes the facts about the cruelty of slavery for Blacks in the United States and the abhorrence of legal discrimination. What these laws will prevent is the deconstruction of the facts of history through a narrow ideological lens of power and oppression to teach an ideology of race-based guilt intent on tearing down America. In fact, these laws will preserve the facts of history from being distorted.

The other objection raised is that these laws are a violation of teachers' freedom of speech. But there is a clearly established legal history showing that teachers do not have unlimited freedom of speech in their capacity as educators. For instance, in 2007, the Supreme Court declined to hear the case of an Indiana teacher who was fired because of the way she expressed her opinion about the Iraq War.[4] "The First Amendment does not entitle primary and secondary teachers, when conducting the education of captive audiences, to cover topics, or advocate viewpoints, that depart from the curriculum adopted by the school system."

In addition to efforts at the state level, we must start paying much more attention to local school board elections. School boards are responsible for determining district curricula and are an important battleground for the future of our country. In recent months, candidates running against Critical Race Theory being used in classrooms have won resounding victories. School board elections are particularly useful because they are usually held independently of statewide and national elections, so a small increase in turnout can be decisive.

1776 Action is one organization fighting to defeat anti-American indoctrination by making it a central voting issue in state and local elections. They're doing it through state-by-state advocacy campaigns and their "1776 Pledge to Save Our Schools" for candidates and elected officials.[5] The pledge is serving as a tool for concerned parents and grandparents to evaluate the men and women who will be helping to make K–12 curriculum decisions. If they can help to elevate the voices of parents and force politicians to clarify their stances on this topic and take action, they can be an effective force all over the country.

Alumni of colleges and universities should find out if and how critical theory is being used and taught at their alma maters and condition donations on what they learn. There are legitimate reasons a school of higher education would include works of critical theory in its curriculum, especially in philosophy or political science courses. But is it being taught as one of many outlooks on the world to be understood academically, or is it being used as a tool for indoctrination, being taught as "the truth"?

It is also important that we are not just playing defense against critical theory and the woke movement. We need an affirmative history and civics education platform that communicates the realities of our history and its impact on today while enthusiastically defending and promoting the core, universal truths of the American experiment that are the source of our success. This platform should affirmatively teach colorblindness as the American ideal, consistent with the Declaration of Independence's assertion that we are "created equal." It should also teach the importance of adopting an American identity that we have in common, not one defined by the color of one's skin.

One wonderful resource that could be used is *Red, White, and Black,* a collection of essays written by Black Americans who reject victimhood and the anti-American worldview of the woke movement by showcasing stories of success. The book is one of many elements of curriculum being developed by 1776 Unites, a project of the Woodson Center.

FIGHTING BIG TECH'S WAR ON FREE SPEECH

The big tech companies are private companies, but there is a long legal history in America of recognizing that when private companies are operating critical infrastructure, they are bound by certain standards of neutrality of access. This is particularly true when these companies receive special protection from the government, as Big Tech does. As I mentioned previously, Section 230 is a protection given to social media and other online content platforms in the early days of the tech boom that made clear they would not be held responsible for the way that customers used their platforms. This helped these companies grow and prosper by removing a big source of risk for their enterprise.

Now these start-ups are giants, and the big tech companies are arguing that they can censor what they want but they also should not be held responsible for any harm that comes from content they allow or suppress. They cannot have this both ways. Either they are a neutral, common carrier or they are editors, similar to a news organization, and can be held liable for the content on their platform.

There is also legal precedent showing that private companies are not allowed to act on behalf of the government in a way that violates a citizen's fundamental rights, such as freedom of speech. After President Trump won the 2016 election, the Democrats and their mainstream media allies blamed online misinformation (and Russia) for the result. This began a coordinated pressure campaign on Big Tech from lawmakers to rein in content they didn't like—a campaign that continues today—using the COVID-19 pandemic and January 6 intrusion of the U.S. Capitol as excuses. The fact that Big Tech has dutifully complied by ramping up their censorship means that they are acting as an agent of the federal government, which is de facto government censorship of speech.

Once again, Congress needs to update (or erase) Section 230 to make it clear that if big tech companies want the legal protection of being neutral, common carriers, they must act like them. It must either be strictly enforced or revoked altogether.

UN-WOKEING CORPORATE AMERICA

One of the most disturbing developments of the past few years has been the rise of the woke corporation. Companies such as Coca-Cola, Major League Baseball, and American Airlines now see it as their job to weigh in on the political issues of the day. We can push back against these companies by understanding the pressures they are facing that cause them to go woke in the first place.

The first reason companies go woke is completely self-serving: relevance. There is enormous competition for attention in the modern media environment. Corporations believe that longtime customers have well-established buying patterns and preferences and are unlikely to change them. Meanwhile, there are new, potential customers out there who because they are younger are more likely to be left leaning. Companies believe that taking a woke stand is a good way to get their attention and develop brand affinity. They are making a bet that going woke will gain them more customers than they will lose.

We can fight back by making sure these companies lose that bet. 2ndVote is an organization that researches the donations of companies to nonprofits and scores them based on how left-wing their donation patterns are. Their argument is that where you spend your dollars is your "second vote" and that you should spend your money on companies that are not hostile to American values.

Another effort under way to make woke corporations pay a price for their left-wing activism is an ad campaign from Consumers' Research. The ads are much like political ads attacking a candidate. The ads accuse companies such as American Airlines, Nike, and Coca-Cola of woke politics as a way to distract from the way they treat their workers or other scandals.[6] The point is: if you're going to play politics, you should expect a political response.

The second reason companies go woke is that the left has weaponized stock ownership. Stockholders are technically part owners of publicly traded companies. This gives them the right to attend shareholder meetings and the ability to file resolutions that can force a vote. Obviously, only a small minority of shareholders ever show up at these meetings, so by organizing left-wing stockholders, the left is able to steer companies in a leftward direction in a way that does not represent the views of all shareholders.

This strategy from the left is quite brilliant and conservatives need to catch up. Stop Corporate Tyranny was established by the Free Enterprise Project and other conservative organizations to beat the left at its own game—and ensure representation of traditional American values at shareholder meetings. I encourage you to visit their website and see how to become involved.

The third reason companies go woke is institutional, and it is more difficult to address. The professional class is overwhelmingly educated at elite universities, which are overwhelmingly liberal.

It should not be a surprise that the elite students that these elite companies are hiring are bringing their elite values with them. This is true not just of the C-suite positions in upper management, but the entire professional managerial class in these companies. This is a problem that begins in the universities and can only be addressed by wresting control of the universities away from the left-wing ideologues.

Boards of directors are increasingly becoming dominated by the left as well. As Justin Danhof, director of the Free Enterprise Project, pointed out in a *Daily Signal* podcast, the left has "co-opted and straight up purchased the search firms that large companies use to identify board members."[7] So, the CEOs of these companies, even if they are not particularly political, receive enormous pressure from their employees and board members to stake out ground in support of liberal causes. Shareholder activism is one way we can insist on ideological diversity on boards of directors.

Regardless of how these companies made the hard turn to the left, their bet is not playing out well. A February 2021 Gallup poll shows Americans' satisfaction with major corporations has plummeted to just 26 percent (from 41 percent in 2020). This was particularly striking given that big businesses helped many Americans through the COVID-19 pandemic crisis. Interestingly, the main cause of the decline came from Republicans, who are likely dissatisfied by corporate virtue signaling over the last year. As *The Wall Street Journal* editorial board wrote on February 5, 2021:

> "The firms believe this is good business, and affluent progressive consumers cheer the new political model. But everyone still gets one vote in elections, and the business community may be making a mistake by aggressively

antagonizing the very Americans it has long relied on to protect it from government control."[8]

DON'T FORGET THE CULTURE

During my time living in Rome, Italy, while Callista was serving as U.S. ambassador to the Holy See, I was fortunate to visit the Vatican museums many times. As you would expect, almost all the works of art displayed in the museums are explicitly Christian. Despite this, every day, tens of thousands of people of all faiths and backgrounds line up to view these great works of Western civilization.

The reason? Simple. They are beautiful. There is something about them that transcends tribal identity and speaks to the human condition. It is a testament to a civilization that it can produce works of such transcendent appeal. The reason the left is trying to discredit the classics is that they suggest there is something about Western civilization worth preserving. This explains why the Biden administration revoked President Trump's order that "classical architecture shall be the preferred and default architecture for Federal public buildings."[9] It is part of the left's belief that cultural hegemony is stopping Marxist revolution that makes them want to discredit and destroy all that came before.

We should use this to our advantage. We should commit ourselves to defending the classics because we know they are worth preserving. We know this because they have survived for this long and must have value that is bigger and stronger than the whims of the moment. Conservatives should refamiliarize themselves with the great works of Western civilization and defend them against the woke mob.

One of the most basic rules of politics that I learned from Ronald Reagan is to stand next to 80 percent issues and smile. There is a similar principle. Stand next to great works of art that have lasted hundreds—even thousands of years—and smile. Show the world what extraordinary beauty the totalitarian left is seeking to discredit and destroy along the way to their glorious woke future.

CHAPTER EIGHT

FREEDOM, WORK, AND PROPERTY

O ne of the greatest struggles in our generation is the fight between those who believe in work enabling self-reliance and those who believe in relying on the government. This split between opportunity and dependency, self-reliance and bureaucratic dependence, is one of the key division points that will define the future of America.

At the end of the movie *Braveheart*, after enduring horrendous torture, William Wallace, with his dying breath, shouts "freedom!" The movie ends with the Scots, inspired by Wallace's courage and dedication, rising and winning their independence. The real Wallace died courageously and became a national symbol. He defiantly argued before his death that he could not be found guilty of treason because no Scot was subject to the crown of England. Wallace's determination in fighting the English for the previous eight years inspired the Scots to reclaim their freedom.

This thirst for freedom was captured in New Hampshire when, in 1809, General John Stark, the most famous New Hampshire soldier in the Revolutionary War, wrote a toast for an anniversary celebration of the Battle of Bennington. That battle mattered because the Americans defeated the British and helped force General John Burgoyne into surrendering—an event that led to a surge of support for American independence. General Stark's toast echoed the sentiments of Wallace when he said: "Live free or die: Death is not the worst of evils." Today, "live free or die" is the New Hampshire state motto.

Thomas Paine captured the cause of freedom in his two widely read pamphlets *Common Sense* and *The American Crisis*. Paine's argument for freedom and justification of the Declaration of Independence in *Common Sense* made it (on a per capita basis) arguably the most widely sold American book in our history.[1] For Paine, the revolution was a moral cause and freedom was at its center.

Being free requires a work ethic and an ability to acquire and maintain property. If you do not have a work ethic you will not be able to acquire property. If you have no property, you must depend on the government for your survival. A government that can decide your fate is the opposite of freedom. You cannot personally guarantee your God-given, inalienable rights "to life, liberty, and the pursuit of happiness" unless you can work and earn property rights (or some other kind of your own capital).

For a long time, the left in America and Europe has worked to make people comfortable with relying on government, getting something for nothing, and being told they are entitled to whatever they want. One of the key tests for the survival of American civilization will be whether we are going to continue to slide into a Bernie Sanders–Joe Biden style of learned helplessness (in which everything is provided to us by bureaucrats and politicians) or whether we are going to reassert core American values and habits of independence and self-reliance.

Do not be confused: Dependency vs. opportunity; work vs. doing nothing; earning your own way vs. other people taking care of you; valuing what you earned (and what others earned) because you know how much time and effort it took vs. assuming everything must be easy because government keeps giving you things without you having to do anything—these are core values that define two different civilizations. One civilization runs on earned freedom with citizens in control of their lives and their government. The other civilization runs on decaying passivity within bureaucratic and elite control.

Historically, America has been deeply and explicitly on the side of earned freedom, and the heart of that is work. Perhaps nothing more clearly defines being American than the work ethic. It is hard to imagine how we could maintain American values if we become a passive, weak, dependent people counting on government to determine our lives.

This belief in work was driven home for me in a presidential debate in February 2012, in Myrtle Beach, South Carolina.

Fox News anchor Bret Baier asked me, "What is the maximum length anyone should be able to collect unemployment checks?"

I said, "Well, you know, Bret, I think there's a better way to . . . think about this. All unemployment compensation should be tied to a job training requirement."

I was suddenly cut off by a thunderous applause. It took me a moment to recover, and I continued:

"If somebody can't find a job and they show up, and they say, 'You know, I need help,' the help we ought to give them is to get them connected to a business-run training program to acquire the skills to be employable. Now the fact is, 99 weeks is an associate degree."

There was more applause.

I kept talking about the value of getting people employed so they could support themselves and I kept hearing more applause.

Then debate panelist Juan Williams, who is a friend of mine, asked me: "Speaker Gingrich, you recently said Black Americans should demand jobs, not food stamps. You also said poor kids lack a strong work ethic and proposed having them work as janitors in their schools. Can't you see that this is viewed, at a minimum, as insulting to all Americans, but particularly to Black Americans?"

I simply responded, "No. I don't see that." I then shared that my youngest daughter's first job was doing janitorial work at the First Baptist Church in Carrolton, Georgia. Then I shared some stories from the people I had heard from while I was campaigning who were deeply supportive of work requirements for welfare and job training for those who couldn't find work. I eventually got back specifically to Juan's initial question and commented that everyone would be better off if schools would hire students to do work for which unions were gouging school systems:

"You could take one janitor and hire thirty-some kids to work in the school for the price of one janitor, and those thirty kids would be a lot less likely to drop out. They would actually have money in their pocket. They'd learn to show up for work. They could do light janitorial duty. They could work in the cafeteria. They could work in the front office. They could work in the library. They'd be getting money, which is a good thing if you're poor. Only the elites despise earning money.

". . . So here's my point: I believe every American of every background has been endowed by their Creator with the right to pursue happiness. And if that makes liberals unhappy, I'm going to continue to find ways to help poor people learn how to get a job, learn how to get a better job and learn some day to own the job."

At some point in this exchange the thousands of people in the Myrtle Beach Convention Center spontaneously responded with a standing ovation in favor of work. It was stunning to sit on the debate platform and see that many people become that excited about a core value. The intensity and spontaneity of the support for work surprised me, but the notion that most Americans believed in work was something I had been sure of for my entire life.

I grew up in a hardworking family that just assumed you would stay busy no matter where we lived. At different points, I worked as a pin setter at a former Luftwaffe bowling alley at an army base in Germany. I babysat for neighbors (my love for dinosaurs began while reading books at a neighbor's house in Fort Riley while I was babysitting). I set sod at the Seventh Army dependent quarters in Stuttgart, Germany. I delivered newspapers, and many other typical teenaged jobs. In addition to the paid activities, my sophomore year in high school I wrote a long paper on the balance of world power. I did my first radio talk shows, and a series of local TV shows my junior and senior years in high school, and I generally stayed busy. The idea of passively waiting around for someone else to take care of me would have been appalling. (My wife, Callista, and my daughters, Kathy Lubbers and Jackie Cushman, have equally strong work ethics.)

My daughter Jackie, whom I mentioned in the South Carolina debate, had also been a waitress on roller skates at Sonic, worked as a bank teller for the People's Bank, and spent a summer at Callaway Gardens selling ice cream. All this before she went to college. So, my faith in the power of work and the importance of work to personal independence grew directly from my life and my family's life.

When we were drafting the Contract with America in 1994, we had been so certain that the American majority preferred work to welfare and opportunity to dependency that we had made welfare reform a major part of the Contract. When the debates about welfare reform were over, the American people were overwhelmingly in favor of a work-oriented reform. In fact, even sixteen years after work requirements were passed, in 2012, 83 percent of Americans still favored them, according to Rasmussen Reports.[2]

The support for welfare reform was so great President Bill Clinton had campaigned in 1992 with a slogan of "ending welfare as we know it." Everyone on the right assumed Clinton meant a more work-oriented system. Everyone on the left assumed Clinton was for spending more money on a bigger bureaucracy. When we brought our work-oriented welfare reform bill up for a final vote, the Democrats split exactly evenly—101 for welfare reform and 101 against.

The language of the opposition on the left was vicious and deeply emotional. They portrayed us as people who were going to destroy children. The left has a deep commitment to promising money without effort. Shifting from a dependency-enhancing welfare system to a work- and opportunity-enhancing system turned out to be amazingly effective. As welfare offices morphed into employment offices, and as the welfare bureaucracy shifted from emphasizing how to get government aid to how to get a job, the results were amazing. The greatest reduction in American childhood poverty came in the three years after welfare reform was passed.

This happened because the amazing success of welfare reform led people to go to work. This increased government revenue as people began earning a living and paying taxes. And it reduced expenses as people dropped off food stamps, got off welfare, began moving out of public housing, and moved from Medicaid to private insurance.

This combination of reduced costs and increased revenue (which affected federal and state governments) was a major factor in our ability to balance the federal budget for four straight years for the only time in your life. Despite the human and financial success of welfare reform, the American left hated it. A work and self-reliance model violated all the core beliefs of redistribution, dependency, and bureaucratic controls.

In its hatred of work requirements, the modern left represents a radical shift in American policies. As Marvin Olasky wrote in his brilliant 1992 book, *The Tragedy of American Compassion*, there was a long tradition in America of tough love toward the poor. There was a deep sense of the deserving and undeserving poor in the American philanthropic tradition. In fact, the reformers who worked with the poor despised (and in some cases hated) the "caring rich" who loved giving away money. Virtually all the nineteenth-century reformers who personally worked with the poor believed that unearned charity was extraordinarily destructive.

This was the driving belief that led to the creation of the Great Depression–era work-not-welfare programs, which reshaped and restored America and saved a generation of Americans from abject poverty.

As Bob Anderson wrote for the *Federalist* on May 20, 2021:

"To address catastrophic unemployment that reached as high as 23 percent, the government constructed millions of jobs through programs such as the Works Progress Administration (WPA) and the Civilian Conservation Corps (CCC). That's not to say the New Deal was a socio-economic panacea (it wasn't), but that in those days people were willing to work to survive. They were offered a hand up, not a hand-out—a concept Democrats still embraced at the time."

Giving a "hand up, not a hand-out" is the absolute key to helping people get themselves out of poverty. Benjamin Franklin captured this spirit at the beginning of the American nation when he said:

"In my youth, I traveled much, and I observed in different countries, that the more public provisions were made for the poor, the less they provided for themselves, and of course, became poorer. And, on the contrary, the less was done for them, the more they did for themselves, and became richer."

This is possibly the most definitive repudiation of the modern welfare state that we have, even though it was written generations before the modern left developed a system of subsidizing and sustaining dependency and indolence. Olasky asserted that a tradition of helping the poor through work, cultural change, and strong measures and language against destructive habits and attitudes was central to helping the poor rise from poverty to prosperity.

The guilt-ridden intellectuals of the modern era were so struck by the difference in the scale of wealth and quality of life between the poor and the wealthy that they adopted policies of wealth transfer and the "right" to an unearned living in which the individual's habits and practices were to be subsidized no matter how destructive they are. We can see the consequences of this destructive policy today in the entire neighborhoods of homeless people on the streets of Los Angeles, San Francisco, Portland, Seattle, and other left-wing cities. In each of these cities, you can find hypodermic needles and other dangerous drug paraphernalia littering the sidewalks and parks. There is a government-maintained website in San Francisco that tracks human feces found in the streets of the city. The radical Democrats who lead these cities are subsidizing desperate, impoverished people as they decay.

In a deep sense, the modern left has been infected by the rejection of earned prosperity captured by Jean-Jacques Rousseau, who said:

"The first man who, having enclosed a piece of ground, bethought himself of saying 'This is mine,' and found people simple enough to believe him, was the real founder of civil society. From how many crimes, wars, and murders, from how many horrors and misfortunes might not any one have saved mankind, by pulling up the stakes, or filling up the ditch, and crying to his fellows: Beware of listening to this impostor; you are undone if you once forget that the fruits of the earth belong to us all, and the earth itself to nobody."

Rousseau's rejection of property (and therefore of earned prosperity) attacks the heart of the American system. Americans have developed a civilization around the belief stated in the Declaration of Independence that we are "endowed by our Creator with certain unalienable rights among which are life, liberty, and the pursuit of happiness." The word "pursuit" is a key component of the Declaration. It is the opposite of the socialist belief that you should be guaranteed and granted happiness by the government.

There could hardly be a greater contrast than the radical rejection of property and the American colonists' avid pursuit of property. The radicals say, as Rousseau said, "the earth belongs to us all." From this vantage point, why should you have to "pursue" a universal right to the earth? The American model is dramatically the opposite of the socialist model of a passive right to happiness provided by government.

As Franklin said, it is "the working man who is the happy man. It is the idle man who is a miserable man." While Franklin wrote about the individual, President George Washington projected the same principle to the entire country, when he said: "A people . . . who are possessed of the spirit of commerce, who see, and who will pursue their advantages, may achieve almost anything." From the earliest days of colonization people came from England, Scotland, Wales, Ireland, and elsewhere to "pursue happiness." There was a widespread consensus that pursuing happiness was the individual's responsibility. It would never have occurred to the Founding Fathers to establish a Federal Department of Happiness.

Our early leaders thought it was self-evident that you should work and strive—and that it was your responsibility to improve your life and improve your family's future. This is because at the time it was a totally unique idea that this was even possible. We were breaking out of an aristocratic, monarchal society. The new American society was one in which people could improve their own lives regardless of who their family was, or where they came from. It is easy to forget looking through a modern lens, but this was a novel and courageous idea at the time.

Coming back to Franklin: His entire lifetime and his celebrity status were a tribute to the rewards of hard work. Beginning with his apprenticeship at age twelve, in which he learned the printing trade, Franklin worked constantly. He published *Poor Richard's Almanac,* which was widely read. He became a world-renowned scientist, a diplomat, a coauthor of the Declaration of Independence, and an ambassador who helped convince the French to support the American Revolution. (Earlier, he had been an ambassador from the colony of Philadelphia to London and was trying to avoid war. But he was rebuffed by the British aristocracy.) Franklin was the oldest member of the Constitutional Convention. His list of accomplishments is almost unimaginable.

Franklin was very clear on the importance of work. At various times, he said:

- "Never leave that till tomorrow which you can do today."
- "Sloth makes all things difficult, but industry all easy; and he that riseth late must trot all day, and shall scarce overtake his business at night; while laziness travels so slowly, that poverty soon overtakes him."
- "Energy and persistence conquer all things."

The legacy of the pioneering farmers, trappers, and traders who opened up America had within a half century created a new and different country—remarkably different from a Europe of kings and peasants.

In the best study of early American civilization, *Democracy in America* (1835), Alexis de Tocqueville wrote:

"It is extremely difficult to obtain a hearing from men living in democracies, unless it be to speak to them of themselves. They do not attend to the things said to them, because they are always fully engrossed with the things they are doing. For indeed few men are idle in democratic nations; life is passed in the midst of noise and excitement, and men are so engaged in acting that little remains to them for thinking. I would especially remark that they are not only employed, but that they are passionately devoted to their employments. They are always in action, and each of their actions absorbs their faculties: the zeal which they display in business puts out the enthusiasm they might otherwise entertain for idea."

If you want a real sense of the decay of America, contrast de Tocqueville's "they are always fully engrossed with the things they are doing" with homeless settlements in Chicago, Baltimore, New York, and other Democrat-run cities with substantial unemployment and astonishing levels of crime.

Consider de Tocqueville's "they are not only employed, but they are passionately devoted to their employments," contrasted with the lack of energy, excitement, or passion found in all too many teachers' union–crippled inner-city schools.

The rise of the welfare state has been a disaster, and the people who are paying the greatest price for these bad ideas are the poor. The Biden administration and its parallel forces at the state and local level have doubled down on the idea that work is virtually irrelevant and that people have no real responsibility for themselves.

The left wants to make poor people comfortable in poverty. This ultimately creates a spirit of passivity as the relative flow of cash and services makes it less practical to go out and take a first job at a low income. The government is willing to pay you more to do nothing than you can earn by going to work.

We are running an empirical test on a national scale. When is the point in which various government programs pay enough so that businesses cannot find workers because government transfers have priced them out of the labor market? States that have eliminated extra unemployment payments from COVID-19 have seen a dramatic shift toward going back to work. States that have maintained the higher government grants have continued to make doing nothing, rather than doing something, more profitable.

Doing nothing is a disaster for Americans. Learning to passively wait for someone else to take care of you is a disaster for Americans. Subsidized passivity is a disaster for Americans.

The answer to these disasters is to create an environment in which it is vital for Americans to learn to be energetic, active, and constantly learning.

This difference is captured powerfully in *Rough Edges: My Unlikely Road from Welfare to Washington* by Judge Jim Rogan. I served in Congress with Rogan and found him to be courageous, hardworking, disciplined, and strikingly smart.

Rogan was born to a single mother who ultimately ended up in prison for a felony. He dropped out of high school in his junior year. He worked at a wide range of jobs and ultimately got a law degree and became a successful prosecutor specializing in gang murders. Judge Rogan knows from personal experience that hard work, constant effort, and a willingness to learn widely (from mentors and practical experience) can enable people to succeed even when the odds are stacked against them.

I first realized what a disaster our modern welfare state was when I interviewed refugees from the American defeat in the Vietnam War. If the refugees got to America and went to work even at a menial job, they rapidly rose and learned to assimilate into American culture. However, if the refugee got pulled into the welfare culture, began living in public housing, and focused on maximizing subsidies from the government, then there was a pretty good chance he or she would learn to be passive and focus on getting more government money rather than focusing on earning more money.

A key part of the sickness of the welfare state is it teaches you to learn how to "get" money rather than how to "earn" money. The difference in the two attitudes has created a growing sickness of theft and corruption.

A good indicator of how sick things have become is the theft that is widespread in the recent COVID bailout distributions. In California, an estimated $31 billion was stolen from the unemployment compensation program alone.[3] Even if you assumed each thief took $100,000, that would require 320,000 people willing to steal from the state of California. Nationwide, authorities believe roughly half of the unemployment money dolled out during the COVID-19 crisis was stolen. That's $400 billion in tax dollars now in the hands of criminals.[4]

A more crime- and corruption-oriented society is a natural outcome of people "getting" money rather than "earning" it. The thin line between "getting" and "earning" is clearly understood by the working poor. They get up every day and go to work. They watch their money carefully because they know what it cost them (not what it cost some anonymous taxpayer). They know that work, honesty, and frugality are keys to their standard of living and quality of life.

The working poor resent (much more than the wealthy) when someone they know cheats and steals. They know it is at their expense and it is inherently unfair. It also rewards really bad behavior. The combination of an illegal economy (drugs, prostitution, theft) and a government safety net that rapidly becomes a trap to enable destructive behavior—including alcoholism, drug addiction, and indolence (a fancy word for laziness)—has corroded much of America's social strength and resilience. The explosion of fentanyl deaths, the scale of the cocaine industry, the size and squalid poverty of the tent cities and other homeless centers—all these are symptoms of the social decay caused by the policies that the "generous" left has supported for at least three generations.

Two of the greatest disasters inflicted by the current welfare state mentality are in policies that have driven males from home and policies that have dumbed down the schools to enable people to feel good about themselves as they fail to learn what they will need to get a job.

The collapse of male presence in the homes of single mothers has left young males with no role models of successful, work-oriented, law-abiding males. The result has been an increase in violence and disorder. This decay into gangs, tribalism, and violence has unwound the core of civilization in all too many poor neighborhoods.

The poor have been crippled educationally by the combination of terrible education policies, bureaucratic decay, the replacement of a passion for helping people learn, to an intense focus on compensation and work rules. Note the teachers' unions fought bitterly to keep unionized public schools closed after the COVID-19 crisis even as Catholic and other private schools were safely opened with in-person learning at virtually no risk. The union-run schools have undermined the potential for the poor to get educated and rise.

The combination of fatherless homes, terrible schools, high crime levels driving out jobs, government subsidies for teenage mothers at the exclusion of male participation, and the tolerance for extraordinary murder and shooting rates in poor neighborhoods have created an American dystopia of the poor.

CULTURE MATTERS

The real disagreement is not about money. It is about culture. The left believes if you transfer money to people who are immersed in a culture of poverty, you have done all you need to do. This is exactly wrong. If you transfer money without effort, you teach people a culture of indolence, poverty, and looking for other people to take care of you.

The adage "give a man a fish and you feed him for a day. Teach a man to fish and you feed him for a lifetime" is a perfect example of the two very different approaches to poverty. The left believes feeding someone every day so they can eat though they remain dependent is an adequate policy.

We believe that is a false charity, allowing people to feel good while doing harm. We believe a policy of expanding independence by teaching people to do things and take care of themselves is true charity, because it leaves the person being helped better off than they were.

Many people have told me they had no money when they were young, but they were not poor. They are making the case that absence of money is not poverty—but learning to be poor can lead to an absence of money and can trap people in poverty. A culture of work leads to a long time horizon, a constant search for learning and self-improvement, the development of networks of friends and coworkers who strengthen the worker's ability to be productive and get things done.

The difference in teaching a twelve- or sixteen-year-old a culture of work and achievement rather than a culture of poverty and dependency may not be gigantic in the short term. The difference over twenty or thirty years between the two lifestyles is astonishing.

People who learn to work enjoy the fruits of their labor. With each passing year their ability to get things done, to work with productive, successful people, and to have bigger dreams with greater skills makes the gap between dependency and independency grow.

THE HOMELESS AND THE CULTURE OF POVERTY

When people come to expect something for nothing, it leads them to indolence. They have all day and no responsibilities. Since they are used to getting something while doing nothing, and they have been reassured that they are "owed" the money for the act of being alive, many of them begin to believe it is their right to be given money.

This system has led to people decaying in boredom and passivity while others become more aggressive in demanding money, committing crime, and stealing from their own neighborhoods.

Imagine that we replaced the liberal dependency system with an earned help system. Imagine that we required everyone to do some work in return for whatever they were given. At its most basic, imagine that the homeless in San Francisco were required to spend time cleaning up their own feces.

Once a civilization begins to decay, it can accelerate rapidly down a steep decline into passivity, indolence, ignorance, and violence. America is now teetering on the brink of that kind of decaying culture. That is why this debate over work vs. welfare, knowledge vs. ignorance, and independence vs. dependence is so vital.

CHAPTER NINE

PEACE, SAFETY, AND STABILITY

After a summer of protests, riots, and looting; the pandemic crisis; and a year of rising crime and violence, America must return to peace, safety, and stability. We must again be a nation of laws rather than mobs, order rather than chaos, and hope rather than despair.

We have a long way to go, but we can get there.

After the horrific killing of George Floyd in May 2020, hundreds of thousands of rightfully outraged people took to the streets in protest. Nearly a year later, Derek Chauvin, the officer who killed Floyd by kneeling on his neck, was found guilty of second-degree unintentional murder, third-degree murder, and second-degree manslaughter. In June, he was sentenced to more than twenty-two years in prison. His attorneys have requested another trial, citing alleged jury intimidation and other factors. The other officers involved are also being tried in the courts at the time I am writing this. In the end, despite Chauvin's wrongdoing, the justice system worked as intended.

But long before the trial, the video that captured Floyd's death had gone viral, and the court of public opinion almost immediately rendered its guilty verdict. In cities across the country, hundreds (and in some cases thousands) of people took to the streets in protest. In some places, protestors were peaceful and exercised their guaranteed right to peaceably assemble and petition the government for a redress of grievances. The national media, which was sympathetic to the cause, constantly reinforced that the protests across the United States were "mostly peaceful."

However, across the nation, radical groups such as Antifa, militant cells of Black Lives Matter activists, and opportunistic criminals took advantage of the crowds and wreaked havoc. Genuine riots broke out in more than 140 U.S. cities, including Chicago, Los Angeles, Minneapolis, New York, Philadelphia, Washington, D.C., and others. Violence continued for more than one hundred days in Portland, Oregon. Six city blocks in Seattle were taken over by militants for a month starting in June. They forced police out of a precinct, vandalized government buildings, and patrolled the area with armed thugs. The National Guard had to be called up in more than twenty states, including the nation's capital. The cost of the destruction, looting, and vandalism from these supposedly peaceful protests from May 26, 2020, through June 8, 2020, was estimated between $1 billion and $2 billion, according to the Insurance Information Institute. It was the most destructive and costly period of civil unrest in American history (although I expect the Civil War truly ranks higher).[1] As the institute reported:

"For the first time, [Property Claim Services] designated the civil unrest in Minnesota and those events that followed across the United States from May 26 to June 8 as a multi-state catastrophe event. This makes the 2020 event the first time since 1992 that PCS has compiled significant insured losses for a civil disorder and declared it a catastrophe. PCS has included more than 20 states with significant losses for this catastrophe. A preliminary estimate of insured losses from PCS which is still subject to further evaluation, would be more than $1 billion, marking it as the costliest civil disorder in U.S. history."

Beyond property damage, in the first two weeks of the protests, nineteen people were killed in cities where mobs were running amok.[2] Many news outlets were quick to report that not all of these people were killed as a direct result of the protests. *USA Today* disputed a comment by conservative pundit Drew Hernandez, who posted on Instagram, "More Black people have been killed due to the George Floyd riots than unarmed Black people fatally shot by police in 2019. This is not progress." The newspaper's fact checker, Adrienne Dunn, explained that while 14 Black people had died during the first fourteen days of protesting—the same as the number of unarmed black men shot by police in 2019—six were either not directly connected to the protests or the connections were still being investigated.

This was nothing more than weaponized pedantry to promote the media's insistence that the protests were "mostly peaceful" and ultimately good for the country. What about the eight Black men who were killed because of the rioting? How many of the six that were still being investigated needed to be found related to the riots before there was a problem? You must also wonder if all these deaths could have been avoided if cities hadn't been in chaos and police had been able to respond to crimes.

At the time of the protests, I wrote that if we want to stop violence in the country, we must stop *all of it*. Yes, we need to seriously look at our policing and our communities to figure out how and why Black men get shot by police twice as often as white men. But more than simply bringing parity between the two statistics, let's work to see how we can build a society in which being shot by police almost never happens—to anyone.

That will take more police training, but it will also take a serious focus on making sure Americans everywhere are equipped with skills and have access to opportunities that allow them to thrive no matter where they grow up.

Further, if we are going to get to that society, we must not allow mobs to roam our streets burning, looting, and vandalizing our communities. How has $2 billion in damage made our cities better? How has it improved the lives of residents? How has it further promoted peace, unity, or equal treatment under the law? The fact is, it hasn't. As I wrote when the first fires started being set in May 2020, the first rule of dealing with riots is simple: you must stop them.

When riots are happening, the rule of law cannot exist. Mobs are led purely by raw emotion. As a result, angry mobs become incredibly dangerous in a short amount of time because the standards of behavior evaporate in the boiling chaos. That is how you create an environment in which normally sane, compassionate, rational people find themselves setting cars on fire, breaking store windows, or throwing bricks at police officers.

So, the only way to prevent this madness is for the forces of orderly society to impose themselves steadily and firmly on the mob. In cities across the country during the Floyd protests, law enforcement and National Guard should have been there in force—and ready to immediately act to quell violence—before the first rock was thrown. Americans have a guaranteed right to assemble, but they must do so peacefully. The moment a mob or protest becomes violent, it is no longer a valid constitutional act of free expression.

And by the way, this is universally true. The mobs that stormed the U.S. Capitol Building in January 2021 were operating under the same paradigm. They were angry, they gathered together, and they were allowed to impose themselves on the undermanned U.S. Capitol Police, who had no hope of bringing order to the crowd. Before the mob even arrived at the U.S. Capitol, every available law enforcement officer should have been surrounding the building—and been prepared to do what is necessary to prevent a mob of criminals from vandalizing and desecrating the sacred halls of Congress.

When order pulls back, chaos moves in—and innocent people are hurt.

THE DEFUNDING FRAUD

Unfortunately, Democrat leaders in most of the cities where the violence was happening were too busy virtue-signaling their support for the mob to ensure the safety of their other citizens. Almost immediately after the protests started leaders across the nation began calling to "defund the police" to appease the mob. While many people describe it differently, the main goal of defunding the police is to move resources out of traditional policing and into social work and other mental health services—although some activists call for simply doing away with police. Public safety groups everywhere cautioned against reducing police in the midst of nationwide protests and a pandemic, and hindsight has tragically validated those concerns.

As Stephanie Pagones reported for Fox News, the Minneapolis City Council in July 2020 first moved $1.1 million out of the police budget and into crime prevention programs. A few months later, in December, council members unanimously approved a budget that had cut $8 million from the city's police department and allocated it toward mental health teams and other efforts. While the cuts didn't directly cut police staffing, this loss of resources deeply demoralized officers—and emboldened criminals in Minneapolis. Adding fuel to the fire, in March 2021, most of the Minneapolis council members publicly voiced support for fully disbanding and replacing the police department.[3] The result: from July 22, 2020, to March 28, 2021, violent crime in Minneapolis was up 22 percent going from 3,025 offenses to 3,692 violent crimes.[4]

This trend continued in state after state. City officials in Portland, Oregon, cut $16 million from the city's police department. Homicides promptly tripled. From July 2019 to February 2020, before the protests, there had been 17 killings in Portland. From July 2020 through February 2021, 63 people had lost their lives. The Los Angeles City Council cut more than $150 million from the police budget in July 2020. Murders in that year were up 38 percent, according to Pagones, and 2021 murders were up 28.3 percent as of March. As the Law Enforcement Legal Defense Fund reported this year, "less policing = more murders." According to the police officer advocacy group, 2020 saw the largest year increase in homicides on record, rising 25 percent nationwide—from 16,000 homicides in 2019 to more than 20,000 murders in 2020.[5]

Clearly, defunding the police is not the right answer—it is the wrong one. It's also profoundly irresponsible and dangerous. Had elected leaders listened to the American majority instead of the loud, angry mobs, much of the destruction and death of 2020 could have been avoided. According to a 2021 survey by McLaughlin & Associates, 80 percent of Americans want to fully fund police and law enforcement. Similarly, Pew Research in July 2020 found that only 25 percent of Americans favor reducing police funding. Meanwhile, 42 percent believe it should remain at current levels, and 31 percent say it should be increased.[6]

Most Americans are for making sure police have all the resources they need, and most Americans are for protecting police officers. McLaughlin & Associates found that 74 percent of Americans support mandatory life sentences for people convicted of killing police officers. And 72 percent support mandatory prison sentences for anyone who physically attacks police officers. The American majority instinctively knows you don't achieve fair policing by slashing budgets and making life more dangerous for civilians and officers. You achieve fair policing by holding police to account. This is why 90 percent of people reported to Pew Research that they support the creation of a federal database that tracks officers who are accused of misconduct.[7] This would prevent problem officers from being able to avoid investigations or consequences for malpractice by moving to another department or precinct. It is also a perfectly rational way to root out bad police officers.

ORDER AT THE BORDER

Another place in which order must be restored soon is our southern border with Mexico. Having safe, rational borders (and an immigration system that prioritizes the well-being and happiness of Americans) has been one of the biggest motivating issues for voters in the last decade. In the 2016 election, Republican voters were driving the argument. They wanted secure borders, tighter enforcement of immigration laws, and to ensure those who were allowed to enter the United States could care for themselves without relying on public resources. As I wrote in *Understanding Trump* in 2017, this was a reaction to eight years of policy and media culture that led Americans to feel as though their needs and hardships were less important than those of noncitizens who were in the country illegally—or trying to be.

Before the recent political era, the idea that we should have a secure, orderly border had been fairly mainstream. As Deroy Murdock wrote for *National Review* in January 2019:

> "Former and current senators: Joe Biden, Tom Carper, Hillary Clinton, Dianne Feinstein, Barack Obama, Chuck Schumer, Debbie Stabenow, and Ron Wyden were among the 26 Democrats who voted for the Secure Fence Act of 2006. It authorized 700 miles of double fence. All 54 Senate Democrats voted unanimously in June 2013 for $46 billion in border security, including 350 miles of new steel fence."

As Murdock reported, Democratic support for a wall at the southern border specifically fell out of fashion in 2015, when Donald Trump became a serious Republican contender for president.[8]

After that point, the elite media and national Democrats consistently dismissed concerns about permissive immigration policy and weak border security as bigotry or xenophobia. After Trump's election, they constantly refrained that the wall on the southern border would not work (even when Department of Homeland Security officials and U.S. Customs and Border Patrol statistics consistently indicated it did work).[9]

They repeatedly advocated for loosening immigration laws and granting citizenship to the nearly 11 million people who were in the country illegally—with almost no conditions or restitution for back taxes or public obligations. And the American left consistently argued that people in the country illegally should receive government-funded health care, public education—and in San Francisco and nine Maryland cities, the right to vote in local elections.[10] Keep in mind, McLaughlin & Associates found in the first months of 2021 that 84 percent of Americans only want citizens to be able to vote in elections.

In the 2020 election, the energy over immigration and border security had shifted. President Trump's zero tolerance immigration policy, and his administration's determination to follow the law that Congress had written—rather than invent or interpret its own—resulted in unacceptable consequences. Children were separated from family members when they crossed the border. Unaccompanied children were put into detention-style lodgings because there were no other facilities to accommodate the volume of people. It was a crisis. At the time, I said so—and I said that the Republican Party cannot be the party of separating children from their parents.

The Trump administration took steps to mitigate the fallout, but it couldn't act quickly enough. Some of the children did not know how to reach family members in the United States. Others who had come over in caravans had no family to whom they could be released and had to stay in federal custody. Because of this, the media, which already hated President Trump, filled airwaves, inboxes, and social media feeds with heartbreaking images of hungry, desperate children who were forced to stay in underequipped federal buildings that were never meant to house children or families in the long term.

There were nearly no pundits or columnists writing about how it was Congress's job to legislate our immigration process—or that the despicable situation was the direct result of U.S. law and a series of activist judicial rulings being followed to the letter. At the same time, the media ignored positive news about illegal border crossings being reduced drastically under President Trump—which meant less human trafficking, fewer people being forced to smuggle drugs into the United States, and fewer people dying of starvation and thirst in the desert. This became an enormous problem for the former president. Throughout the 2020 election cycle, Democrats no longer needed to argue or debate the virtue of having a secure border. They didn't have to argue or debate anything about immigration. The media did all their campaigning for them.

Once Biden was elected, the national media became less horrified about seeing young immigrant children in detention facilities. At the same time, the number of unaccompanied minors in federal custody exploded.

As CNN reported in April 2021:

"Earlier this month, unaccompanied migrant children spent an average of about 122 hours in Customs and

Border Protection custody, longer than the 72 permitted under US law, according to data obtained by CNN.

"By the end of March, the number of unaccompanied children held up in Border Patrol custody peaked at nearly 6,000. At the height of the 2019 border crisis—when there were overcrowded facilities and children sleeping on the ground—there were around 2,600 unaccompanied children in Border Patrol custody, a former US Customs and Border Protection official told CNN."[11]

You read that correctly. When President Trump was charged by the media with a record number of immigrant children in federal custody, the number was 2,600. We saw a months-long media campaign smearing the president, Republicans, and anyone who was for a secure border. Biden's record was 6,000, and we got minimal, obligatory coverage, in which Democrats were quoted without question or cross-examination. Of course, the Biden administration's immediate answer to this problem was simply to bar media from seeing the facilities or reporting on the crisis.

As the Associated Press reported on March 26, 2021:

"News organizations say they have repeatedly sought access and been blocked. The Associated Press, for example, has asked Homeland Security officials for access to Border Patrol facilities at least seven times, without a response. The Biden administration has pointed to the need to establish safeguards for COVID-19 transmission and protecting the privacy of children as they work to set up their system for processing migrants."[12]

Plenty of other news outlets raised their hackles over not being allowed into these facilities. As CNN reported the same month, "The Biden administration has so far denied journalists access to border facilities amid a surge of unaccompanied minors crossing the US-Mexico border, which has raised questions about its commitments to increased transparency."[13]

But note the important difference in tone. This wasn't about the welfare of beleaguered children or moral outrage over their treatment. It was about the media's access and privilege. President Biden's answer to dealing with the border crisis—and the media pressure—was to pass responsibility for the U.S. border to Vice President Kamala Harris in March, who did little about it for more than three months. By June, the crisis at the border had reached historic levels.

As Axios reported: "The number of migrants illegally crossing the U.S.-Mexico border this fiscal year is already the most since 2006—with four months left to go, according to preliminary Customs and Border Protection (CBP) data."[14]

By then, Harris had still not visited the U.S.-Mexico border, instead opting to travel to Guatemala. In an interview with NBC's Lester Holt, she told him she sought to deal with the root causes of mass migration to the border—corruption and violence in some Central and South American countries. Aside from a few days of stories about Harris's perplexing response to Holt when he asked her why she hadn't yet visited the southern border (she noted that, "and I haven't been to Europe"), the national press quickly pivoted to stories that were less critical of the Biden administration. Under pressure, she eventually visited the border in June.

The southern border (and immigration in general) is yet another area of policy on which Democrats are completely ignoring the American majority. If every member of Congress was listening to the American majority, we would see legislation passed that reformed our immigration system so that America attracts people with skills and education rather than simply encouraging family reunification (74 percent of Americans supported a focus on work and skills in the McLaughlin & Associates survey). Yes, we are a nation of immigrants, but that has never meant that we should have (or ever had) open borders and admitted any person who wanted to enter the country and become a citizen.

A highly permissive immigration policy can lead to glutted or lopsided labor markets, which can lead to more wealth disparity, poverty, and potential for crime. American immigration policy should focus on what skills our economy needs and accept people who can provide those skills. What we cannot afford to do is to accept people who do not have the skills or ability to contribute to society or take care of themselves.

This is why the American majority's immigration bill would also end taxpayer-funded giveaways such as welfare, health care, and free college tuition for people in the country illegally (no giveaways has 75 percent support of Americans, according to the McLaughlin & Associates survey). Now, of course, there are desperate people who come to the United States seeking asylum. I'm not arguing that they should all be turned away—or allowed in with no assistance. However, the American majority does not want America to become the world's safety net. It would become an open-ended magnet attracting millions. We simply can't afford it.

Finally, an American majority's immigration law would be incredibly tough on people who enter our country illegally and then seek to break the law. The cross-border drug trade, human smuggling, and slavery are some of the most egregious humanitarian crises in modern times—and all of them are currently happening in America today. All also depend in part on having a porous border that can be easily penetrated by ruthless people. As Mark Moore reported in the *New York Post* in March 2021, the criminal cartels that run human smuggling operations across the U.S.-Mexico border were making as much as $14 million per day in February 2021, when masses of people were seeking to cross the border.[15]

For those defenders of the Biden administration's abysmal handling of the border who argue that human smuggling is not the same as human trafficking, consider what ultimately happens to the vulnerable children who are smuggled and dropped off across the border. As Texas governor Greg Abbott has pointed out, unaccompanied children who are smuggled across the border are at high risk of being ensnared in human slavery and the sex trade. Abbott has sought to remedy the disaster Biden and Harris have left at the border by expanding Operation Lone Star, a state program that pledged 1,000 Texas Department of Public Safety officials to help Border Patrol investigate possible human trafficking cases.

As Abbott said on March 17, 2021:

> "President Biden's reckless open border policies have created a humanitarian crisis that is enriching the cartels, smugglers, and human traffickers who often prey on and abuse unaccompanied minors. . . . Whether it's securing the border or fighting human trafficking, the state of Texas will always step up to fill the gaps left by Washington."

Any serious American majority-focused immigration law would tighten our borders in a way that particularly targets drug smugglers, human traffickers, and other dangerous people who seek to take advantage of lax border security. People who are caught illegally crossing the border would be promptly investigated for these horrendous crimes and prosecuted if they were suspected of committing them. Any noncitizen gang members who are arrested by police within the country would be immediately deported (this had 87 percent support in the McLaughlin & Associates survey).

Whether you are in the middle of the country or at the border, our civilization cannot survive without order. We must return to being a nation of laws—not men or mobs. The laws must apply to everyone—and they must be enforced upon everyone. This was one of the most basic concepts enshrined in our founding—and it's something the American majority still deeply supports.

PART III

PROTECTING THE AMERICA WE LOVE

CHAPTER TEN

RENEWING AMERICAN LEADERSHIP

For the past 245 years, the great American experiment has thrived and enabled generations of Americans to pursue their American dreams, push the limits of science, explore unknown frontiers, and create breathtaking masterpieces. Since 1945, the United States has been at the forefront of innovation, economic development, military strength, and advancing human rights. America has led the world in championing individual freedom, democracy, and the rule of law.

But today, the United States faces significant threats to our strength, security, and values. Some of the most pressing foreign policy challenges directly impact Americans' security and livelihoods. For instance, the economic challenge with China has deeply impacted the lives of America's workers, businesses, industries, and consumers while jeopardizing the security of our supply chains. The Biden team is enacting an energy policy that makes America energy dependent, kills American energy jobs, benefits our adversaries, raises costs for American consumers, and puts our economic and national security at risk. A failure to defend against and deter inevitable cyberattacks will leave our critical infrastructure, industries, and the privacy and security of Americans vulnerable to attack at any moment. Communist China is challenging universal human rights on the international stage to further the power and prestige of the totalitarian dictatorship that poses a direct threat to our fundamental values.

For America to remain the strong, shining city on a hill and a beacon of freedom and liberty for the world, we must work to address these key challenges threatening our country and our values. Obviously, health care is a major target for improvement and reform—and a potential opportunity for American leadership. I wrote several chapters on improving health care in my last book, *Trump and the American Future*. Since that plan still holds up, I direct you there.

DEFENDING HUMAN RIGHTS

Individual freedoms, liberty, and human rights are at the heart of what it means to be an American. It is no surprise then that the American majority and lawmakers oppose the oppression and abuse inflicted by the Chinese Communist Party—one of the world's most egregious violators of human rights—against its own people. According to a poll by McLaughlin & Associates, 73 percent of Americans support promoting free and democratic elections, and human rights in China.

As I wrote in *Trump versus China: Facing America's Greatest Threat* with my coauthor Claire Christensen, China is controlled by a communist totalitarian dictatorship that prohibits free speech and democratic elections. It denies citizens due process, violates religious freedom, and oppresses minorities. For decades, the United States incorrectly assumed that China's communist totalitarian system would evolve into one that was more free and more open. But we were totally wrong. As Human Rights Watch reported in January 2021, today is the "darkest period for human rights in China since the 1989 massacre that ended the Tiananmen Square democracy movement."[1]

For example, in June 2020, the Chinese Communist Party eliminated the freedom and autonomy of Hong Kong with its imposition of a new national security law. The broad-sweeping, ambiguous law, intended to crack down on dissent and punish opposition to the Chinese Communist Party, gives Beijing the power to imprison Hong Kongers for life for any act of alleged secession, subversion, or collusion with foreign actors.[2] In the aftermath, prodemocracy candidates have been disqualified from election, activists have been arrested and jailed, and Hong Kongers who attempted to flee to Taiwan were caught and jailed.[3]

Further, the Chinese Communist Party is "Sinicizing" religion by regulating, prohibiting, and controlling religious beliefs and practices. China is designated by the United States as a Country of Particular Concern—which is defined as a country in which the government has "engaged in or tolerated systematic, ongoing and egregious violations of religious freedom."

As my wife, Callista Gingrich, the former ambassador to the Holy See, wrote in a May 2021 article, "In China, religious freedom and belief threaten the Chinese Communist Party's total control and authority in the country. As a result, the Chinese Communist Party continues to persecute people of faith and exert control over religious practices."[4]

The Chinese Communist Party is also rampantly committing genocide against the predominantly Muslim Uyghurs and other members of ethnic and religious minority groups in Xinjiang.[5] The CCP has imprisoned at least 1 million to as many as 3 million people in concentration camps, where they are forced to pledge loyalty to the Party, praise communism, learn Mandarin, and renounce Islam.[6, 7] Highly concerning reports of horrific living conditions, torture, sleep deprivation, sexual abuse, rape, and suicide have emerged from survivors of the camps.

The Chinese Communist Party closely watches those living in Xinjiang and has instituted population controls. Xinjiang has been transformed into what's been termed an open-air prison. The Chinese Communist Party has created a digital surveillance state that monitors and tracks residents in the region, while "minders" are assigned to live with Uyghur families.[8] Uyghurs have also been subject to forced abortion, sterilization, birth control, DNA collection, and unexplained medical tests.[9, 10] Moreover, Uyghurs both inside and outside of the camps are forced into systematized slave labor. An Australian Strategic Policy Institute report titled "Uyghurs for Sale" first exposed serious concerns that forced labor in Xinjiang had permeated the supply chains of major global brands in March 2020.[11]

Recently, the tomato and cotton industries have been making headlines for risks associated with sourcing materials from Xinjiang that could be made with slave labor. Consequently, the United States banned tomato and cotton imports from Xinjiang by issuing a Withhold Release Order on January 13, 2021.[12]

But, based on China's trade data, Xinjiang's top export to the United States for 2020 was not tomatoes or cotton. It was wind turbines. Xinjiang Goldwind Science & Technology Co.

Limited, commonly known as Goldwind, is the largest wind turbine manufacturer in China. In 2020, Goldwind ranked number two (behind General Electric) for the company with most commissioned wind capacity in the world.[13] As the name would imply, the company is based in Xinjiang, which raises concerns that its products could be made using forced labor. Microsoft bought forty-eight wind turbines from the French energy company Engie, to install in southwest Texas as part of its goal to use 100 percent renewable energy by 2025.[14] After reviewing shipping data, customs records, and corporate documents, *The South China Morning Post* found that Goldwind supplied wind turbines for the project.

Similarly, Xinjiang provides approximately 40 percent of the world's polysilicon—a material refined from rock that is used to make solar panels. A report by the consultancy group Horizon Advisory found that some of the major solar companies in Xinjiang have shown signs indicative of forced labor practices, including government-facilitated work transfers and forced "military-style" training for the workers. The companies identified by Horizon Advisory account for a total of more than one-third of the global polysilicon supply.[15]

The United States has taken bipartisan action to stand up in opposition to the Chinese Communist Party's horrific human rights abuses. For example, Congress passed into law the Hong Kong Human Rights and Democracy Act in November 2019,[16] the Uyghur Human Rights Policy Act in May 2020,[17] and the Hong Kong Autonomy Act in July 2020.[18] Moreover, both the Trump and Biden administrations determined that the abuses committed by the Chinese Communist Party in Xinjiang constitute genocide.

Despite these known, explicit examples of institutionalized, state-sanctioned human rights abuses, Communist China was chosen as the host for the 2022 Winter Olympic Games. The Chinese Communist Party will undoubtedly seize upon this opportunity to exploit all of the international prestige that comes with hosting the games—while promoting its vision for a "community with a shared future for mankind" (read: CCP-led world order). But based on the extent of the horrors that the CCP is inflicting upon its own people, Communist China has no business hosting this celebration of human achievement.

At the time of this writing, the International Olympic Committee has resisted pressure to move the Winter Games. President Biden, meanwhile, has offered what *The Washington Post* accurately described as "confusing and contradictory signals" about what to do regarding the games.[19] This is a tragically weak response. The United States, as the world's leading voice on freedom and human rights, should demand with our allies that the International Olympic Committee move the Games out of Communist China.

The atrocities in Xinjiang have been condemned by members of Congress from both sides of the aisle. Though a diplomatic boycott of the Beijing games has received strong bipartisan support in Congress, this approach doesn't go far enough to address the clear and evident genocide taking place at the hands of the Chinese Communist Party.

Representatives Michael Waltz (R-FL), Guy Reschenthaler (R-PA), and John Katko (R-NY) introduced a resolution in February that called for the International Olympic Committee to rebid the 2022 Winter Olympic Games.[20] Barring the success of moving the Games, the resolution calls for a U.S.-led international boycott.

Representative Waltz also introduced a bipartisan bill with Representatives Tom Malinowski (D-NJ) and Jennifer Wexton (D-VA) that would prohibit any federal contracts for four years with businesses that sponsor the CCP-hosted Winter 2022 Olympic Games.[21] Federal buildings and military bases would also be prohibited from selling these businesses' products.

Cochairs of the Tom Lantos Human Rights Commission, Representatives Chris Smith (R-NJ) and James McGovern (D-MA), said that the United States cannot turn a blind eye to the genocide and carry forward with "business as usual." Smith warned, "In granting Beijing host status for the Olympic Games, we are crowning a barbarous regime with laurels while we should be condemning their abuse and genocide." Postponing the Games to give the International Olympic Committee more time to find a different location makes total sense, according to Representative McGovern. "If we can postpone [the Tokyo] Olympics by a year for a pandemic," McGovern said, "we can surely postpone an Olympics for a year for a genocide."[22] Boycotting and relocating the Olympics will send a strong message to President Xi Jinping and the Chinese Communist Party regime that the United States and our allies will not stand by and maintain the status quo while the dictatorship commits genocide against innocent minorities.

Additionally, the United States needs to ensure that we are not enabling the continued atrocities in Xinjiang by allowing the risk of slave labor to corrupt our supply chains. Senators Marco Rubio (R-FL), Jeff Merkley (D-OR), and their Senate colleagues reintroduced the Uyghur Forced Labor Prevention Act in January 2021.[23] The bipartisan House companion bill was introduced in February 2021 by Representatives McGovern (D-MA), Smith (R-NJ), Thomas Suozzi (D-NY), Vicky Hartzler (R-MO),

Tom Malinowski (D-NJ), Mike Gallagher (R-WI), and Wexton (D-VA).[24] This important bill would establish a "rebuttal presumption" that all goods sourced from Xinjiang are made with slave labor. As a result, these goods are banned from coming to the United States without "clear and convincing" evidence that shows no slave labor was used in production.

The situation in Xinjiang is opaque, but as more details emerge from testimonies of courageous survivors, and the work of activists and researchers, the pervasiveness of the Chinese Communist Party's state-sanctioned slave labor is overwhelming. A boycott of the Beijing Olympics and the passage of the Uyghur Forced Labor Prevention Act are necessary steps to ensure that the United States does not allow the CCP to benefit from abusive labor practices and genocide.

PROTECTING OUR JOBS AND SUPPLY CHAIN

Communist China's infiltration into U.S. supply chains carries significant risks in perpetrating human rights abuses in China. However, Communist China's control over critical industries also directly threatens critical U.S. economic and national security interests. According to a February 2021 Gallup poll, China is viewed by Americans as the United States' greatest enemy.[25] Additionally, a record 63 percent of Americans asserted that China's economic power is a critical threat to the United States. An additional 30 percent view China's economic power as an important threat, bringing the total to a whopping 93 percent of Americans that see China's economic heft as a threat to the United States. This rising concern among Americans is well warranted. Since 2001, 3.7 million American jobs have been lost to

China.[26] Less than ten years later, in 2010, Communist China overtook the United States as the world's dominant manufacturer. In 2019, China was the source of 28.7 percent of the world's global manufacturing output, according to the United Nations.[27]

The Chinese Communist Party intends to expand and strengthen its preeminence as the hub of global manufacturing. The government's Made in China 2025 plan, for example, identifies ten critical advanced manufacturing sectors that the Chinese Communist Party intends to dominate. These sectors include: new generation information technology; new energy and energy-saving vehicles; high-end computerized machines and robots; energy equipment; aerospace; agricultural machines; maritime equipment and high-tech ships; new materials; advanced railway transportation equipment; and biopharma and high-tech medical devices.[28]

Further, economists have estimated that Communist China's economy will overtake the United States as early as 2026 or, more conservatively, by around 2032.[29, 30] But China has not become a major global economic player by playing by the rules. Rather, the Chinese totalitarian dictatorship has violated international rules, annually stolen hundreds of billions of dollars in intellectual property, manipulated its currency, and provided government subsidies to domestic industries.

According to a report released in June 2018 by the White House Office of Trade and Manufacturing Policy, "Much of [China's] growth has been achieved in significant part through aggressive acts, policies, and practices that fall outside of global norms and rules."[31] The report also noted that Communist's China's "leading position in many traditional manufacturing industries" was achieved "in part through preferential loans and below-market utility rates as well as lax and weakly enforced environmental and health and safety standards."

Americans want to bring our jobs back stateside. According to a poll by McLaughlin & Associates, 87 percent of Americans support "Made in America" tax credits for businesses making their products in America. Further, the poll also found that 82 percent of Americans support requiring fair trade with Communist China to bring back manufacturing jobs to the United States.

Communist China's economic aggression ultimately threatens the U.S. economy and has eliminated American jobs and industry. One of the clearest examples of the communist Chinese dictatorship hollowing out American industry can be seen by looking at the once-flourishing and now nearly extinct U.S. solar industry. Between 2012 and 2017, more than two dozen U.S.-based solar cell manufacturers were forced to close as a result of the Chinese dictatorship's subsidizing and dumping of artificially inexpensive products into the marketplace—shrinking the U.S. industry by 80 percent. In 2017, a 4–0 ruling, the U.S. International Trade Commission determined that U.S. solar manufacturers were significantly hurt by China's subsidies.[32]

Tariffs imposed by the Trump administration and International Trade Commission anti-dumping duties helped to bring back some of the U.S. solar panel manufacturing industry. In 2019, U.S.-made solar panels hit a ten-year record 19.8 percent of market share.[33] President Biden has pledged to install more than 500 million solar panels nationwide and said, "When I hear the words 'climate change,' I hear the word 'jobs.'"[34] Climate czar John Kerry meanwhile has assured laid-off oil workers that they "can be the people to go to work to make the solar panels."[35] These statements

RENEWING AMERICAN LEADERSHIP

don't point to a reasonable plan. Instead, they show just how disconnected leftist elites are from the American majority.

The reality as it stands today, is most of the solar industry jobs will be in Communist China. First, eight out of ten of the world's top solar companies are based in China.[36] In the United States, almost 80 percent of solar panels that are installed come from Communist China's companies.

But we need to look further down the supply chain to understand China's grip on the solar industry. For context, highly purified silicon, or polysilicon, is transformed into ingots, which are then ground and sliced into thin wafers. Solar wafers are then used to make the solar cells that, when connected together, form a solar panel. China controls 64 percent of the world's polysilicon material, while the U.S. market share is a mere 10 percent. China also controls almost 100 percent of the solar ingot and solar wafer global market. The vast majority—80 percent—of the world's solar cells are also manufactured in China, while the United States' share is in the single digits.[37]

Communist China's domination of manufacturing and supply chains threatens not only American jobs and the economy, but also U.S. national security. In addition to the solar industry, China has also secured control over the world's rare earth industry. As Dr. Larry Wortzel and Kate Selley concluded in a brief for the American Foreign Policy Council's Defense Technology Program in April 2021, "The United States has been caught off guard by China's dominance of the rare earth industry. Over the years, the US has become dependent on a potential adversary for some of the most crucial materials in high technology production: rare earth elements."[38]

Though the name implies otherwise, rare earths are not rare. In fact, these elements can be found in deposits globally, including in the United States. Rare earths include 17 different elements: cerium, dysprosium, erbium, europium, gadolinium, holmium, lanthanum, lutetium, neodymium, praseodymium, promethium, samarium, scandium, terbium, thulium, ytterbium, and yttrium. Rare earths could be as indispensable as oil as they are critical for high technology production.

Rare earth elements are important in the production of cell phones, computer hard drives, medical imaging equipment, electric vehicle motors, and wind turbines. These elements are also essential in the manufacturing of critical military technology. For example, a Congressional Research Service report from 2013 noted, "[E]ach SSN-774 *Virginia*-class submarine would require approximately 9,200 pounds of rare earth materials, each DDG-51 Aegis destroyer would require approximately 5,200 pounds of these materials, and each F-35 Lightning II aircraft would require approximately 920 pounds of these materials."[39]

Between the 1960s and 1980s, the United States led the world in the production of rare earths. Communist China has since secured dominance in this industry via the refining and extraction of rare earth elements—due to its weaker labor and environmental laws. As a result, China produced 63 percent of the world's rare earth production in 2019 and supplied 78 percent of U.S. imports of rare earths.[40]

According to Wortzel and Selley, the Mountain Pass Mine in California is the only rare earth metals mine that is operational in the United States, though others are being developed.[41] Mountain Pass accounts for approximately 10 percent of all rare earth concentrate. However, at the time of this writing, Mountain

Pass doesn't process its materials—no U.S. firm does—so the rare earth concentrate is sent for processing (metal extraction) to China. (As a note, the Trump administration's Department of Defense issued a $9.6 million award in November 2020 to add processing and separation capabilities to Mountain Pass.)[42]

American vulnerabilities that are caused by a reliance on Communist China for rare earth elements gives the Chinese Communist Party a significant strategic and political advantage— of which the dictatorship is well aware. Take the case of Japan in 2010, for example. Japan and China both have laid claims to the disputed Senkaku Islands (which China calls the Diaoyu Islands) in the East China Sea. After a Chinese trawler near the islands collided with two Japanese Coast Guard patrol ships, Japan arrested the trawler's captain to put him on trial. In an "apparent retaliation" for the Chinese captain's detention, China embargoed rare earth material exports to Japan.

The dangers of the reality that Communist China controls critical components of the U.S. defense and consumer technology supply chains cannot be overstated. As Wortzel and Selley wrote, "Today, U.S. industry, the military services, the Executive Branch and Congress are learning lessons that should have been obvious earlier, when the PRC used rare earth elements as a weapon against Japan. First, the United States needs to know the supply chains for the production of vital products. Second, the U.S. cannot depend on a single source for vital materials. And third, it cannot put its industrial base at the mercy of an increasingly arrogant and hostile potential enemy."

However, it's not just rare earth elements that China has come to control. In 2018, the U.S. Department of the Interior published a list of thirty-five mineral commodities that had been identified as being critical to our economic and national security (critical minerals).[43]

The rare earth elements, in addition to arsenic, gallium, indium, graphite, tantalum, bismuth, antimony, barite, magnesium, germanium, and tungsten, were some of the minerals included on the Department of Interior's list of critical minerals. What do all of these minerals that are used for near infinite applications—from defense and renewable energy capabilities to semiconductors, integrated circuits, batteries, fuel cells, medical and atomic research, cement, fiber optics, and steel manufacturing—have in common? In 2020, the United States was a net importer for more than half of the supply of each of these minerals (100 percent net import reliant on foreign sources for arsenic, gallium, graphite, indium, rare earths, and tantalum).[44] Can you guess who was the United States' largest supplier for every single one of these minerals? If you guessed China, you'd be right.

Time is of the essence. The *Financial Times* reported in February 2021 that China's Ministry of Industry and Information Technology put forward draft controls to limit exports of rare earths.[45] Communist China's control over the supply chains of critical minerals and high-tech manufacturing industries pose significant threats to the U.S. economy and national security. These threats require a robust American response to bring back domestic manufacturing and ensure the security of our critical supply chains.

Two administration officials told Reuters at the time of this writing that President Biden's approach to addressing the critical mineral supply chain vulnerabilities will be focused on sourcing the majority of materials from our allies and processing them domestically.[46] Biden's politically motivated priority to appease environmentalists will rob Americans of the opportunity for good-paying jobs, the chance to renew the U.S. mining industry, and fully secure the U.S. supply chain. As Reuters noted, "The plans will be a blow to US miners who had hoped Biden would rely primarily on domestically sourced metals, as his campaign had signaled."

This approach simply doesn't make sense. First, the most effective way to create a reliable supply chain is to utilize American-owned resources that are in safe locations. Second, the best way to create a responsible supply chain is to have jurisdiction over the process so that we can ensure that environmental and labor standards are upheld. Locating the process in other countries without the same level of standards as the United States green-lights bad practices and sends the consequences to other countries, while claiming to "save the environment."

America can't assume that we will have sufficient access to feedstock that we are competing with other countries to obtain. The United States also has a dramatic lack of processing capability, so Biden's strategy is not viable unless economic and environmental goals are pushed back by twenty years. We ultimately need to find a path to reconcile Environmental Protection Agency standards and the permits that are required to be able to process our own material.

Evolution Metals Corporation is an American company that aims to be part of the solution by creating secure and reliable supply chains for critical minerals that will support the economic and environmental strategic goals of the United States. The company foresees domestic industrial ecosystems developing around electric vehicles, green technology, electronics, and defense capabilities and are working with companies that are prepared to participate.

Why should the United States rely on another country for the supply of critical raw materials, when it can be done in the U.S.? This same question of "Why go somewhere else for resources when we have what we need right here, in the United States?" also applies to another industry that is key to the U.S. national security—energy.

MAKE AMERICA ENERGY INDEPENDENT AGAIN

Under President Trump, America was energy independent for the first time in sixty-two years.[47] However, the Biden administration has sought to undo these successes in the name of tackling climate change. President Biden has ultimately taken an energy policy approach that has made the U.S. energy dependent, killed American jobs, increased costs for consumers, and benefited our adversaries.

Consider the following actions and proposals by the Biden administration. As of June 1, 2021, according to *The Washington Post*, President Biden has added 22 new environmental policy "protections" (read: regulations) and proposed 11 more.[48] He has also overturned 34 of the Trump administration's rollbacks and targeted 68 additional rollbacks.

As I mentioned earlier in this book, this all began on President Biden's first day in office. Through executive order, President Biden canceled the Keystone XL pipeline project, which would have led to 26,100 indirect and direct jobs according to a State Department study.[49] One week later, he signed another executive order that indefinitely suspended new oil and gas leases on public waters and lands. (A Louisiana federal judge later issued a preliminary injunction saying the administration does not have the authority to issue this mandate without congressional approval.)[50] But in May, President Biden waived sanctions to enable the completion of the Nord Stream 2 pipeline, which transports natural gas from Russia to Germany. This decision ultimately strengthens Russia, weakens the United States, and does not accomplish any reasonable goal within the realm of American interests.

As I mentioned earlier, President Biden has also said he intends to install half a billion solar panels in the United States. Recall that the country who presently dominates the solar industry is not the U.S., but China. Biden additionally wants to double offshore wind production by 2030. The country that currently dominates the wind turbine industry is, also, China. General Electric is the world's leading global wind turbine maker and commissioned 13.53 gigawatts of wind capacity in 2020. But out of the top ten global wind turbine makers for 2020, companies in Communist China secured seven of them. Considering there is no such thing as a truly private, independent company in China, these seven companies totaled 45.66 gigawatts of commissioned wind capacity for 2020. (The aforementioned Goldwind ranked second behind GE, with 13.06 gigawatts commissioned in 2020.)[51]

Here's the bottom line: By 75 percent the American majority supports maximizing our oil and gas production to keep the U.S. energy independent, according to a survey by McLaughlin & Associates. Yet the Biden administration's actions and regulations are destroying a once-thriving American industry and making the United States energy dependent once again. In 2019, petroleum was the top source of energy consumption in the U.S., accounting for 37 percent of total energy consumption.[52] Unfortunately, in February 2021, the U.S. Energy Information Administration (EIA) projected:

> Throughout much of its history, the United States has imported more petroleum (which includes crude oil, refined petroleum products, and other liquids) than it has exported. That status changed in 2020. The U.S. Energy Information Administration's (EIA) February 2021 *Short-Term Energy Outlook* (STEO) estimates that 2020 marked the first year that the United States exported more petroleum than it imported on an annual basis. However, largely because of declines in domestic crude oil production and corresponding increases in crude oil imports, EIA expects the United States to return to being a net petroleum importer on an annual basis in both 2021 and 2022.[53]

The Biden administration continues to pursue unrealistic "pipe" dreams that, as of today, will only benefit our adversaries and harm Americans.

In a 1984 speech to the Republican National Convention, UN ambassador Jeane Kirkpatrick said that the Democrats had become the "blame America first" party. The Biden administration has taken this even further—from "blame America first" to punish America first.[54] Not only have the Biden administration's policies killed jobs, but they have also made energy more expensive. As I mentioned earlier, the week before President Biden took office, gas was priced at $2.40 per gallon, yet during the week of June 7, 2021, gas cost $3.13 per gallon. In fact, at the time of this writing, the price of gasoline is higher than at any point during the Trump administration.[55]

As House representative Garret Graves (R-LA) said in April 2021, the Biden administration is modeling the national climate agenda after disastrous Californian policies.[56] California's liberal policies have failed at keeping energy prices low for residents, at making the state energy independent, and at reducing emissions. The average gas price in California as of June 7, 2021, was $4.10 per gallon—$0.98 more per gallon than the national average.[57] Electricity in California (when not subjected to blackouts and brownouts) is also much more expensive than the national average. Further, California imports more energy and electricity than any other state.

Increasing regulations and restrictions to curb emissions have proven to be an inefficient model for success. For example, the Obama/Biden administration introduced the Clean Power Plan regulation that required emission reductions in the power sector of 32 percent below 2005 levels by the year 2030. Under this plan, the government would have been calling the shots, which would have raised utility bills, killed jobs, and stifled American competitiveness. The Trump administration halted the rule, and instead, pushed for market forces and innovation to lead decision making as opposed to government regulations. In the absence of the Clean Power Plan, the emission target was achieved—more than ten years ahead of schedule. In 2019, the power sector reached reductions of 33 percent below 2005 levels.[58]

Today, 79 percent of primary American energy consumption comes from fossil fuels.[59] Demand for fossil fuels—which have thirty times the energy density as the next-closest renewable energy source—is expected to increase significantly, especially in developing countries.[60] The United States produces the cleanest and best energy in the world. Ceding energy production to our adversaries with lower environmental standards is a nonsensical approach to a global issue. Take Russia, for example. According to Representative Graves, "Russian natural gas exports to Europe have 41 percent higher lifecycle greenhouse gas emissions than US LNG exports to Europe. The EU gets 30 percent of its gas from Russia." Also, Graves noted, "Russian natural gas exports to China have 47 percent higher lifecycle greenhouse gas emissions than US LNG exports to China."[61]

Clearly, these facts didn't matter when the Biden administration decided to step aside and allow the completion of the Nord Stream 2 pipeline. Incorporating clean, efficient, and cost-effective sources of renewable energy is not a partisan issue. And destroying the jobs of hardworking Americans who made the United States energy secure and independent also shouldn't be a question of partisanship. Increasing regulations, hiking up costs for American consumers, and giving our adversaries the upper hand are not sustainable solutions for the economy, the environment, or our national security.

The United States is the world's leader in reducing emissions and dramatically outpaces the rest of the globe in investing in research and development of clean energy technology. And contrary to what the mainstream media reports, Republicans do in fact support clean energy initiatives. For example, the bipartisan Energy Act of 2020 provided an innovation road map to scale up and bring American clean energy technology to market.

According to ClearPath, a conservative conservation group, "The Energy Act modernizes and refocuses the Department of

Energy's research and development programs on the most pressing technology challenges—scaling up clean energy technologies like advanced nuclear, long-duration energy storage, carbon capture, and enhanced geothermal. Crucially, across all of these technologies, DOE is now empowered to launch the most aggressive commercial scale technology demonstration program in U.S. history. The bill sets up a moonshot of more than 20 full commercial scale demos by the mid-2020s. It also sets ambitious goals for America to maintain global leadership and increases key clean energy program authorizations by an average of over 50 percent over the next five years."[62]

Building upon the momentum of the first energy policy modernization package in more than ten years, House Republicans released an Energy Innovation Agenda that Minority Leader Kevin McCarthy affirmed "won't kill American jobs or make American energy more expensive."[63] The plan focuses on targeted legislation to promote innovation, clean energy infrastructure, and initiatives for natural solutions and conservation. Ultimately, this plan puts the American people first by developing and building new technology in the United States that is affordable, clean, and exportable.

The Energy Innovation Agenda includes dozens of different bills and solutions that will benefit the economy and the environment, while ensuring the security of American energy. Some of the policies include securing the domestic critical mineral supply chain, expanding reforestation, promoting nuclear energy abroad, and streamlining slow and cumbersome regulatory processes for energy projects.

Writing for *The Hill*, American Conservation Coalition vice president of government affairs Quill Robinson outlined three reasons why the Republican plan is the right approach.[64] First, the plan is actionable. Robinson noted that a substantial number of the plan's legislative proposals had already been put forth in Congress with bipartisan support. Second, he wrote that the plan has urgency. The agenda is not a lofty, unrealistic, "all-of-the-above" approach. Rather, it will have real impact in the immediate term, namely through streamlining of regulations that will enable private sector investment.

Last, and most important, the Republican plan appeals to Americans, who are often overlooked in the left's discussions about energy and the environment. Robinson wrote, "While a vast majority want action . . . many are understandably skeptical of sweeping climate plans that will make heating their homes and putting food on the table more expensive. An incremental approach, which doesn't sacrifice American jobs, is a truly bipartisan approach."

THE INVISIBLE WAR

America is currently fighting an invisible war—and has been for quite some time. At every second of every day, government entities, private businesses, and American citizens are all targets. This war doesn't rely on tanks, artillery, or armies in the traditional sense—but rather, lines of malicious code.

The United States has teams of incredibly talented, skilled, and highly trained individuals in the public and private sector who fight this war on our behalf. A lot of the time, they are successful in defending against state-sponsored and private thugs who attempt to exploit America's cybersecurity vulnerabilities.

Recently, however, there have been numerous high-profile cyberattacks that have threatened our national security.

For example, in December 2020, a hack that targeted SolarWinds, an information technology company, was discovered. The corrupted software update gave the hackers access to as many as 18,000 of SolarWinds customers.[65] About one hundred companies and nearly a dozen U.S. federal agencies—including the Treasury, Justice Department, Energy Department, Pentagon, and the Department of Homeland Security's Cybersecurity and Infrastructure Agency—were compromised in what Microsoft president Brad Smith called "the largest and most sophisticated attack the world has ever seen."[66]

The United States has attributed the attack to Russia's Foreign Intelligence Service (SVR), the KGB's successor. But as John Pescatore, director of emerging security trends at the SANS Institute, said, "Russia went beyond 'conventional espionage' in the SolarWinds attack, much the way crashing a commercial jet into the Pentagon goes beyond 'conventional warfare.'"[67] The Biden administration issued sanctions against Russia for its involvement in the attack and expelled ten Russian diplomats.

To be fair, due to the nature of cyberwarfare, we shouldn't assume that we know all of the actions that have been taken by the Biden administration to respond to the SolarWinds attack. It is now clear, however, that the administration's seen and unseen responses weren't tough enough to deter further Nobelium attacks (Microsoft's name for the SolarWinds hacking group believed to be run by Russia's SVR).

On May 27, 2021, Microsoft warned they "observed cyberattacks by the threat actor Nobelium targeting government agencies, think tanks, consultants, and non-governmental organizations." Though 3,000 email accounts at more than 150 organizations were targeted, at the time of this writing, Microsoft had not seen "evidence of any significant number of compromised organizations."

Notably, however, Microsoft assessed, "These attacks appear to be a continuation of multiple efforts by Nobelium to target government agencies involved in foreign policy as part of intelligence gathering efforts."[68]

Foreign adversaries conducting cyberespionage or attempting to hack or corrupt critical U.S. systems are not novel threats, nor are they unexpected. The scale, sophistication, and (the largely unknown) extent of the SolarWinds hack, however, are at the forefront of U.S. national security concerns. According to a Gallup poll, 82 percent of Americans view cyberterrorism (which Gallup defines as "the use of computers to cause disruption or fear in society") as a critical threat to U.S. vital interests.[69] More respondents view cyberterrorism as a critical threat than the development of nuclear weapons by North Korea and Iran, international terrorism, and Russia's military power.

Notably, this poll was taken in February 2021—before two additional high-profile Russian cybersecurity attacks occurred that made the reality of this threat all the more evident.

The first is the May 7, 2021, Russia-based DarkSide ransomware attack, which shut down the Colonial Pipeline for six days. The Colonial Pipeline transports gasoline, diesel, jet fuel, and other refined products to New Jersey from the Gulf Coast, totaling approximately 45 percent of the East Coast's fuel supply. Faced with uncertainty surrounding the extent of the attack and how long it would take to bring the pipeline back online,

CEO Joseph Blount authorized a bitcoin ransom payment totaling $4.4 million (the Justice Department has since recovered $2.3 million).[70] Speaking of his decision to pay the ransom, Blount said it was a choice he didn't make lightly. He admitted that he "wasn't comfortable seeing money go out the door to people like this." Even though it was a controversial decision, he said, "It was the right thing to do for the country."[71]

Even though President Biden issued an executive order following the SolarWinds and Colonial Pipeline attacks to shore up our nation's cybersecurity, another ransomware attack shut down nine beef plants in the United States. The attack targeted JBS, the largest meat supplier in the world, which processes almost one-fourth of U.S. beef and one-fifth of U.S. pork. The FBI determined that the Russian ransomware hacker network REvil, one of the world's most profitable cyber-criminal gangs, was behind the attack.[72] Again, the company was forced to pay a ransom of $11 million in bitcoin to the criminals.[73]

These ransomware hacks illustrate the significant vulnerabilities within U.S. food and energy supply chains and the consequences that adversaries can exploit. Ciaran Martin, former head of the British government's National Cyber Security Center, outlined the three main problems contributing to the ransomware crisis: "One is Russia sheltering organized crime. A second is weak cybersecurity in too many places. But the third, and most corrosive, problem is that the business model works spectacularly for the criminals."[74]

As of this writing, the Biden administration's response to these attacks has been ineffective and a weak slap on the wrist in proportion to the direct threat to U.S. national security that each of these three hacks presented. On June 3, 2021, one former government official described the administration as, "Right now, they are hair on fire."[75]

It should deeply concern us that a private security firm— who was also a victim in the SolarWinds hack—happened to discover one of the largest cyberattacks in history before the U.S. government. It should infuriate us that an American CEO was faced with the impossible choice of hurt Americans or pay criminals millions of dollars. It should trouble us that criminals were empowered to then launch ransomware attack against the world's largest food processor and were successful—again.

There is a real cyberwar that is under way and each of these three attacks was an act of war that directly threatened U.S. national security. Hacking into at least nine U.S. federal agencies is an act of war. Shutting down 45 percent of the East Coast's fuel supply and bringing U.S. beef production to a halt are acts of war.

The United States needs to deal with these virulent attacks accordingly. First, no hackers should be paid any ransom money as a reward for the crimes they commit. Second, the United States needs to make it clear that we will attempt to extradite the hackers and imprison them for life, or that they will be tracked down and eliminated. A great country cannot permit adversaries to attack our systems, jeopardize Americans' livelihood, threaten our national security, and damage U.S. corporations, without any consequences. It is not an effective model to pay off criminals, clean up their mess, then wait for them to come back and do it all over again.

If the risks for hackers do not outweigh the rewards, the United States will continue to be the target of even more cyberattacks. We are on the verge of having our entire system and society undermined. America needs to get tougher with adversarial hackers, or we risk dramatically losing this invisible war.

The challenges that I have outlined have a real impact on Americans and, as the polling has shown, are significant areas of concern. The United States cannot employ half measures to address the critical threats to our economic strength, national security, and our values. We must renew American leadership in the world.

CHAPTER ELEVEN

AMERICAN SURVIVAL IS AT RISK

When you see scenes from Beirut, Kabul, or Caracas, remember that our cities could be as devastated and as poverty stricken. Also understand that it could take only one disastrous attack to move Americans into a terrifying time.

To maintain peace, how do you prepare for war in a time of extraordinary change? As the Roman writer Publius Flavius Vegetius Renatus wrote in the late fourth century, "If you want peace, prepare for war." But if war itself is constantly evolving, for what exactly are you preparing?

The world is changing rapidly and there are emerging threats that could individually or collectively threaten the survival of America. Survival is not just a strong word. The patterns that are building make it possible for the United States to be defeated in a variety of ways that could permanently change who we are and of what we are capable. Our freedom could easily disappear under the dominance of new forces that believe in authoritarian or totalitarian government. Our prosperity could be shattered in a series of attacks from small countries who specialize in building weapons of mass destruction and mass disruption.

The American national security challenge is unique because it has so many different types of threats. No country in history has tried to cope with the wide variety of threats that are clearly on the horizon as America prepares to meet twenty-first-century challenges.

General David Perkins, while he was head of the Army's Training and Doctrine Command, captured the challenge with this scenario: Suppose that he had been appointed in 1980 to study the kind of army we would need in twenty-five years. Remember that 1980 was the peak of the Cold War with the Soviet Union and the army was overwhelmingly focused on winning the key battle in Germany with heavily armored units.

Now imagine that he had produced a report that said the greatest threat in 2001 would be a group of partially trained terrorists seizing four civilian airliners and flying them into our tallest skyscrapers, the Pentagon, and the U.S. Capitol (with only the latter being missed as a result of the courage of the American passengers). Imagine further that in response to this attack (which cost more lives than any assault on American soil including the surprise attack on Pearl Harbor) that America would decide to send nearly 100,000 troops halfway around the world to the landlocked country of Afghanistan to hunt down the terrorists and block any future attacks.

In 1980, this report would have most likely been regarded as harebrained fantasy or warmongering. The key lesson, Perkins concluded, was that we needed an extraordinarily flexible and adaptable military—precisely because we don't (and probably can't) know what future threats will materialize.

This spirit of "Thinking about the Unthinkable" (to use the title of Herman Kahn's 1962 book) must be carried far beyond the army. The entire national security system, including virtually every element of government and a lot of the private sector, must be involved in a new, profound, and deep rethinking of our national security system. It is hard for us to take seriously the process of "thinking about the unthinkable," because our experience has largely been one of containing war and dominating the definition of the wars into which we have been pulled.

The fact is: America has had a remarkably safe and secure existence. Part of the shock of the September 11, 2001, terrorist attacks was the fact that it occurred on American soil. We have had such a strong history of being invulnerable to foreign attacks that even the prospect of a relatively small attack was shocking. The loss of 2,977 lives in one morning on American soil seemed unimaginable until it happened.

However, compare our 9/11 losses with 1.1 million Soviet and 800,000 German casualties at Stalingrad or the Blitz against London in 1940—which killed 43,000, destroyed or damaged 1.7 million buildings, and left one out of every six Londoners homeless at one point or another.

Americans have been fortunate because our military power was multiplied by the fact that we could shelter behind the Atlantic and Pacific. The English Channel, which had protected Britain from a successful invasion for 955 years (since 1066), is at its narrowest only twenty-one miles across. Compare that with the thousands of miles America has sheltered behind on its east and west coasts. Because of our geographic advantages, the size of our economy, our scientific and technological advantages, and the organizational and decision-making capabilities of our political system, we have almost always projected power to fight away from home.

All that may be about to change in devastating ways. The fact is our homeland is now more vulnerable and more exposed than at any time since the British burned the White House in 1814. In real terms, America is at much greater risk than it was in the War of 1812 or any other war since the revolution. The dangers are increasing because our elites, including our military and national security elites, have been lying to themselves about the decay of the international system and its rules, the scale of terrorism, the rise of new forms of conflict, and the game-changing nature of new technologies, new doctrines, and new weapons of mass destruction and mass disruption.

The history of warfare is a constant cycle of offense or defense being dominant. In the Middle Ages, defensive castles were dominant until artillery was developed that could batter them into submission. In World War I, the machine gun and artillery created a stalemate until the airplane and the tank reopened mobile warfare. In both world wars, submarine warfare was a constant back-and-forth between the submarine dominating the ocean and then antisubmarine systems dominating.

We seem to be entering a period in which offense has the advantage. As I mentioned in the previous chapter, the recent hacking into the Colonial Pipeline cutting off 43 percent of the gasoline on the American East Coast was an offensive victory for which we apparently had no defense. When the Chinese Long March 5B rocket became uncontrollable in 2021, and a 22-ton rocket was gradually falling back to earth, President Biden's secretary of defense announced that there were no plans to shoot it down even if it was headed for an American city.[1] This is a good reminder that there is no effective anti-missile defense tested and fielded. Even a small country like North Korea or Iran could likely hit the United States. Even the most successful anti-missile system in the world, the famous Israeli Iron Dome, can be overwhelmed if enough rockets are fired at it. Saturation firing can drown any current system of missile defense.

The current challenges are many: electromagnetic pulse (EMP) weapons, cyberwarfare, biological weapons, artificial intelligence and robotics (in which Russia and China are heavily investing to dominate the American conventional forces), and the potential of a breakthrough that allows one country or another to dominate space. Regardless of which challenge arises, the offensive side for the moment has both a technological and financial advantage. For example, an EMP weapon would be relatively inexpensive. Hardening the entire grid so it could survive an EMP attack would be incredibly expensive.

If you look at the time and money spent on planning and executing the 9/11 attack, the cost-to-benefit ratio is massively in favor of the terrorists. The 19 terrorists who died took nearly 3,000 innocent people with them while more than 10,000 were wounded. The tactical victory of offense on 9/11 was only the prelude to the strategic victory of drawing the United States into Afghanistan. As of today, the United States has been in Afghanistan for nearly twenty years, the longest war in American history. In that time, more than 2,300 Americans have been killed, more than 20,000 Americans have been wounded, and more than $2.4 trillion has been spent.

Despite the longest war in our history, we have not been able to defeat the Taliban. In fact, President Biden closed Bagram

Airfield in the dead of night and left it to be looted before the Afghan government could even secure it.[2] When we leave in full, it is almost certain the Taliban will gradually assert control over most—or even all of the country—with a terrible (and bloody) repression of people (namely women) who have been dramatically liberated by the United States and Western forces.

If we had instead diverted the $2.4 trillion spent on Afghanistan to space, cyberwar, EMP, and advanced robotics, we would both have created an enormous domestic industrial advantage over China and would have given America military dominance for at least another generation. What is even more sobering about the American response to 9/11 and Afghanistan has been the inability of the military and the broader national security system to think through the lessons of failure and defeat.

This has been a continuing pattern beginning with the end of the Vietnam War. As Lieutenant Colonel John Nagl reported in his book, *Learning to Eat Soup with a Knife* (a phrase from Lawrence of Arabia explaining the difficulty of anti-guerrilla warfare), the U.S. Army entered Vietnam with no real sense of how to win a guerrilla war. Over a decade later, we left Vietnam in defeat and still with no notion of how to win a guerrilla war. Nagl felt that the army wasn't even aware there were lessons to learn or different strategies and tactics to apply.

Similarly, Colonel Harry Sommers wrote *On Strategy: A Critical Analysis of the Vietnam War* after a revealing conversation with a senior North Vietnamese officer. Sommers asserted to the officer that the Vietcong never defeated Americans on the battlefield. The North Vietnamese responded bitingly that it was irrelevant, because America still lost the war. Since Saigon is now Ho Chi Minh City, there is a lot of proof that the United States lost the war. That conversation inspired Sommers to turn to the great German theoretician of war, Carl von Clausewitz, whose great work, *On War*, is the most widely read Western book on how to think about wars (its counterpart in China, from 500 BC is Sun T'zu's *The Art of War*).

Sommers's critique of the American way of war emphasized that its tactical and operational brilliance fell apart at the level of strategic planning. Americans were doing what we did well—tactics and operations. We were so busy doing what we did well, and so happy succeeding in the tactics and methodology that fit our culture and bureaucratic structures, it did not occur to us to ask if that was actually the right thing to be doing.

Similarly, Marine colonel Bing West wrote a stunning book, *The Village*, about what worked and what failed during his time in Vietnam. Since 1972, he has written endlessly about what rules of engagement lead to victory in small war environments.

It is painful to read Nagl, Sommers, and West and realize how little our great bureaucracies have been able to adapt. The entire system of *The American Way of War: A History of United States Military Strategy and Policy* was outlined by Russell Weigley. In his remarkable book, Weigley explains a great deal of our strengths and weaknesses.

If we can find a decisive battle of annihilation, the odds are pretty good we can win it. We can plan brilliantly for logistics, project power across the globe, acquire air and space superiority, maintain speed of information superiority, and use immediate tactical advantages at almost every level.

America today is remarkably good at the recognized *tasks* of war, and we would get high grades for completing each task. However, if completing the tasks did not lead to victory, we would be in trouble because we do not think through the failures and invent new tasks quickly. Nor do we equip and train for them with any great agility.

AND THEN WHAT?

In more than forty years of working with professional military education, one of the most important principles I have tried to drive home is: "And then what?" Almost all of America's problems have come in the "and then what?" phase of combat planning.

We had plenty of combat power to drive Saddam Hussein out of Kuwait in 1990–91. After all, we were moving forces that had been designed to defeat the Soviet army in Western Europe. Our investment in high-end technology and training made it virtually impossible for the Iraqis to defeat us—or even slow us down.

We launched an air campaign on January 17, 1991, and ran it against Iraq. In more than 100,000 attacks and 88,500 tons of munitions, the allied coalition decimated the Iraqi infrastructure. The dominance in the air was absolute. As a result of the massive bombing campaign, Iraqi morale collapsed. By the end of the first day, more than 10,000 Iraqi soldiers had surrendered. The campaign ended in four days.

While the results of the 1991 coalition campaign against Saddam were impressive (and I was certainly one of those rejoicing in America's total military dominance), it is possible that they taught us exactly the wrong lessons—and that we have been paying for it ever since.

The greatest lesson was our unchallengeable ability to project power virtually anywhere in the world with remarkable efficiency and accuracy. A Russian general, just a few years after the collapse of the Soviet Empire and the four-day land war, said to an American general I knew that the Soviets could not even have found the airfields. The idea that you could project power that far, that fast, was simply beyond Russian capabilities. In that same meeting, my friend showed the long-distance accuracy of the M1A1 Abrams Main Battle tank on a training range. With its modern optics, it can kill an enemy tank beyond 8,200 feet. The Russian was appropriately impressed, and my friend added a little sales touch: "You ought to see our young soldiers; they shoot much better than an old guy like me."

The early 1990s may have been the peak moment of American power. Russia was still reeling from the collapse of the Soviet empire. China was only beginning to build up its military capabilities. The United States spent more on defense than any competitor by a huge margin. We had developed stealth technology, extraordinary communications and information capabilities, and had a virtual monopoly on space capabilities.

I watched through the 1990s as the big institutional defense systems avoided thinking creatively about the changes that were building and the challenges that were just beyond the horizon. In all too many cases, bureaucratic and lobbying imperatives were crowding out serious military thinking. "What's good for my service" or "what's good for my company" had crowded out asking "what is good for my country." The result was tragic as the gap between the Chinese and American military and national security thinking grew wider.

For the last twenty-plus years, Americans have allowed bureaucratic and corporate interests to define far too much of American military thinking and planning. This has led to inadequate weapons, priced far too high and delivered far too slowly.

The sheer size of the big bureaucracies, their corporate allies, and their lobbyists has made it almost impossible to focus on new strategies using new capabilities in new systems. When you have the biggest defense budget in the world producing an amazing array of technologies and a meritocracy that promotes really smart people (but people who are promoted within the models of the recent past) you have a tendency to constantly reinvent models with which you are already comfortable.

If you are in a time of relative weapons stability, such a strategy is survivable. However, if you are living in a time of dramatic innovation, you face totally different challenges. The leadership of General George Marshall in profoundly changing the pattern, rhythm, and structure of the American military in World War II is a good example of the scale of change we need today.

Marshall had the advantage that military revolutions were occurring all around him: the impact of the German blitzkrieg, the shock of Japanese carrier-based aviation at Pearl Harbor, the continually evolving submarine campaign for control of the Atlantic, the stunning rate of technological change (look at aircraft in 1939 and 1945 or the evolution of tanks in the same time period), the transition from a largely horse-drawn military (the German Blitzkrieg of 1940–42 was horse drawn) to the totally truck- and jeep-powered American and British divisions of 1944. This was a new world and it meant that Marshall had the winds of change at his back.

Yet, Marshall still had powerful colleagues opposing reality and clinging to the world that was disappearing. Consider the case of Chief of Cavalry Major General John K. Herr, who in 1938 said, "We must not be misled to our own detriment to assume that the untried machine can displace the proved and tried horse."[3] On another occasion, Herr said, "Anybody who wants to ride in a tank is a damn fool. He ought to be riding a horse."[4] After German armor had swept across Poland, Belgium, and France, General Marshall asked him to explain how the cavalry was going to adjust to German armored warfare. Herr reassured him that the U.S. Cavalry had studied the Blitzkrieg carefully and believed the solution was to buy horse trailers so the cavalry could get to the forward edge of battle and still be fresh. Marshall listened in apparent total disbelief. He retired Herr and abolished the chief of cavalry's post, according to Colonel David Johnson (U.S. Army, ret.) in *Fast Tanks and Heavy Bombers: Innovation in the U. S. Army 1917–1945*. Johnson was trying to understand the impact of doctrine on the development of the remarkably effective American military of World War II.

A major factor in the speed and modernization of the World War II military was the willingness to retire or reassign officers who no longer had the drive and energy to meet the speed and complexity of the modern world. As Assistant Secretary of War Robert A. Lovett looked back, he commented there was so much "deadwood" in the War Department that it was "a positive fire hazard."

Brilliant leaders such as General Dwight D. Eisenhower were rising rapidly because General Marshall and others were united in their determination to retire the incompetent, tired, and those who simply could not understand the demands of modern war. On at least one occasion, Marshall got a call from a friend of more than three decades asking if he could have three or four weeks to move to his new post because he wanted to stay and help his wife pack. With great sadness, Marshall retired him that afternoon.

I am taking this much time on the personnel aspects of modernizing a system because it is the key to success. If people in office refuse to modernize, recognize that the world is changing at blinding speed, and don't push every day just to stay competitive with China and Russia, we will fail. If we allow them to remain in office when they are incapable of executing, nothing else can be effective in getting the job done. Keeping someone in office who is "good enough" may be the prescription for American defeat in the next few decades.

There are two major zones of unending innovation that will challenge the American system in the next decade: technological change and doctrine, especially at the level of national security rather than defense. These two areas of innovation will impact each other in synergistic ways we have not even begun to understand.

First, on technological change. It is clear from the rate of innovation in artificial intelligence, quantum computing, materials technology, biological knowledge, and robotics that we are living in an age of dramatic change. This requires rethinking and radically experimenting with a host of capabilities. Since many of the most powerful game-changing breakthroughs come from the synergistic interactivities of a number of seemingly unrelated breakthroughs, it takes a whole new approach to conceptualize and organize experiments that bring in widely diverse capabilities.

For example, if an adversary can close down all of our ATMs and block all our citizens from getting money, how much political pressure does that country create for the United States? Similarly, if a foe simply hacks and posts everyone's bank account, so everyone knows what everyone else is worth and what they are spending money on, how much disruption does that cause?

While these two examples are relatively benign and don't have an immediate risk of harming people, what if our opponent decides to take a major hospital and freeze all its medical records, leaving the staff and patients with no way of knowing who is supposed to get which medicines?

One of the great problems with American military planning is that it translates every breakthrough into a relatively narrow military application—and often further shrinks the innovation by limiting it only to doctrinally approved examples. Eisenhower and General George Patton discovered this in 1920 when they tried writing about the potential for armored warfare and were both told they would quit writing this radical stuff or their careers in the army would be over.

Herman Wouk, in the novel *The Caine Mutiny,* recounts a story he knows was true, because he was the young ensign in the training program described in the novel. Wouk had been reading *The New York Times* about the German submarine war against merchant shipping. When the chief petty officer teaching a class said the submarine was a fleet attack vessel and is not used in merchant warfare, Wouk couldn't resist. He asked how it was possible that Germans were sinking hundreds of merchant ships if the submarine was not used in merchant warfare. The grizzled veteran looked at him and said, "Son, in this navy there is no campaign against merchant shipping—got it?" The rigidity makes for an amusing story in a novel, but the underlying reality that doctrine can simply ignore facts is a major threat to American capabilities and potentially to American survival.

The challenge of adapting to new technologies is often compounded because breakthroughs in technology often require breakthroughs in doctrine. In June 1940, the French had more and better tanks than the Germans, but they had two failings that were catastrophic. First, because the Germans wanted optimum mobility, they had put a radio in every tank. Wherever the unit commander was, he had a radio and could command the entire unit. Second, the French tank doctrine had been dominated by the infantry. They wanted slow tanks scattered among infantry units and focused on helping the infantry break through. The result was that fast-moving concentrated German tanks could defeat French units that had better equipment but a crippling doctrine. Ironically, the one French armored unit that decisively defeated the Wehrmacht was the Fourth, led by Charles de Gaulle. He had been a leading advocate of armored warfare and proved that with good leadership and the right doctrine the French could have defeated Germany in 1940.

Doctrine had a similar destructive effect on British armor in the early years of the war. The leading British advocate for maneuver warfare, General Percy Hobart, got into so many fights with the infantry and artillery branches that he designed armored divisions that had too many tanks and not infantry and artillery. The unbalanced nature of the British armored divisions meant that, particularly in the desert of North Africa, the German combined arms teams would simply smash up the British armored units. As an example of tactical innovation, a major breakthrough for the Germans was taking their amazing 88mm anti-aircraft gun and converting it into the most feared tank-killing weapon in World War II.

At the tactical level alone, we will face hundreds of innovations driven by technology. It will be frustrating because our absurdly bureaucratic acquisition system is so paper-bound that it often cannot field a desired technology within the life cycle of the innovation still being new. However, as hard as we will work at the development of tactical innovations, the much more important and difficult task is coping with Russian and Chinese doctrinal innovation at the level of the entire national security system. If we are defeated in the near future, short of a nuclear war, it will be because of the inability to cope with these two strategic developments.

The Russian development is less radical, so let's start with the Russian concept of "hybrid war." One of the greatest challenges in trying to cope with hybrid warfare as a doctrine is its absolute disregard of the rule of law. Essentially, the Russians believe they can and should do whatever is to their advantage. If piously supporting the rule of law is better for Russia, then they should do it. If flagrantly violating every international norm and agreement is beneficial to Russia, then they should do that. It is the pragmatic measure of results that reshapes the principles on a daily or even hourly basis. Some of this reflects President Vladimir Putin's own background as a KGB-trained operative in Eastern Europe. Other measures come out of centuries of Russian history and the disdain of Western liberal democracies by Russian elites for virtually all of Russian history. Some comes purely from the toughness and corruption of so much of the Russian governing class—from the czars to the modern oligarchs.

In a sense, the development of "hybrid war" reflects a Russian understanding that nothing they do makes them "acceptable" to the West. Putin created an expensive Winter Olympics at Sochi in 2014 (including substantial corruption as the government threw money at the project). Putin was determined to cap his efforts to create a new better Russia out of the ruins left by losing the Cold War. He lavished money on the construction and opulent food and drink. This was, in a real sense, the Putin stepping-out party.

And no leaders from the West came. In fact, President Barack Obama went out of his way to appoint gay athletes to represent the United States, in response to intense anti-gay laws under Putin. Russia's Olympic reputation was already suffering since its athletes accounted for more than a third of all the athletes in the world who had been suspended for doping. Two weeks after his Olympics humiliation, Putin occupied Crimea. Seen from the West, it was a horrible breach of the international norms that had dominated since World War II. When Saddam had occupied Kuwait, it led to a massive coalition determined to expel him and reassert the principle that countries don't simply invade each other anymore.

All the armchair experts on TV and brilliant analysts at various state departments and foreign ministries had forgotten a couple of key principles that history had made prominent even if modern political science classes didn't. First, international norms require a nation or group of nations willing to enforce the rules. Saddam's Iraq was small, and he was personally disliked (and therefore easy to isolate). Saddam had no one in his corner defending his right to invade a neighbor. By contrast, Putin's Russia is still a major power. It may no longer be a peer competitor to the United States, but its assets are formidable. It has an estimated 4,407 nuclear weapons. Virtually all of them are on modern delivery systems. By comparison, China has about 350 nuclear weapons. There is an enormous deterrence effect in pressuring a country with 4,407 nuclear weapons.[5]

At the nonnuclear level, Russia has the third most advanced weapons development and manufacturing system in the world. In a number of specialized areas, it is as good as or better than the United States and China. Its hypersonic missiles are superb. Its submarine fleet is formidable. Its ability to project military power long range is second only to the United States. Russia is simply too powerful to be confronted the way Iraq was. Putin knew that.

Second, a great deal of power relies on the strength, toughness, and determination of the person in charge. While Western analysts prattle on about "incentivizing" (usually meaning bribery in one form or another) there is no evidence that Putin places much value on Western "carrots." Putin is like the man who has every reason to be noisy and aggressive in the country club bar on Friday night. Since he knows he will never be accepted by the club's elite as a full member, he might as well enjoy himself at their expense.

Many years ago, during KGB training, Putin took Machiavelli's dictum to heart. Machiavelli warned that there is "greater security in being feared than in being loved." One of the patterns that Western analysts find hard to understand is the Putin technique of publicly hunting down and killing his political opponents. In one case in London, the poison used (which contained the radioactive material polonium-210) was an extraordinarily deadly and rare product. It is believed only one factory in Russia produced enough quantities of it to weaponize.[6] In fact, I think Putin's decision to use that particular poison was a deliberate decision to say to the dissidents and their supporters around the world: "I will hunt you down and kill you without regard to the conventional thinking of your precious international community."

Because there is no overarching rule of law limiting Putin's options, he can opportunistically raise or lower the stakes in pursuing incremental victories. Since there is no real supervision of

Putin within Russia, he is free to increase and decrease risks as his personal instinct suggests. In a very real sense "hybrid warfare" is a rheostat that can be turned up or down quickly and without warning. All around the periphery of the Russian state there are hot spots to be harassed, opportunities for expansion or for interference with neighbors, places where old grudges can be settled, and weak regimes that can be drawn further into the Russian orbit.

It is difficult for the American system to keep up with the rhythm of the Putin model. We must broadly obey the law. We must develop a consensus that a particular struggle is worth the effort. Putin's mission in part is to keep America off balance. If we are occupied elsewhere, he can take bigger risks. If we have thought through what he is doing and moved our forces and our allies to block him, the threat often seems to fade away. However, the threat never completely disappears because Putin always has forces in being and is always looking for opportunities to extend his influence and his interests.

Hybrid warfare includes a wide range of techniques Americans have normally refused to mobilize. In Ukraine, Putin has used criminal gangs reaching even into the capital city of Kiev.[7] In Estonia, Latvia, and Lithuania, Putin has used cyberweapons to punish governments when they fail to do what he wants.[8] He has sent in forces, equipment, and financing to help Assad survive in Syria.[9] In return, Russia sustains a warm-weather port in Latakia, giving Putin a chance to be a real player in the eastern Mediterranean.[10]

In addition to maintaining an aggressive but constantly changing policy along the Russian periphery, Putin has turned more and more to a de facto alliance with China. Russia has an enormous amount of land and resources. The Chinese Communist Party dictatorship has plenty of people but inadequate natural resources. The growth of the Chinese economy has created an environment in which there is a natural system of mutual strengths. Chinese science and technologies are rapidly becoming world class. In some areas—such as hypersonic weapons, space, opening up the Arctic, deep undersea development, applying scientific and technological breakthroughs to next-generation weapon systems, and developing human-biological interfaces with a daring approach to mixing DNA and other processes—no Western liberal democracy can match them.

Two giant power systems with a mutual opposition to the United States defining the world and working together to further their own countries while limiting the American future could be formidable opponents. If over the next two decades the occasional tactical cooperation grows into routine cooperation and planning, then a Chinese-Russian alliance could become a painfully real threat to American security.

One of the added complexities of trying to cope with Russian and Chinese strategies is that they are profoundly different. Working to understand the Chinese rhythm and system does not prepare you for dealing with the Russians or vice versa. Russia's "hybrid strategy" is tactical, often short term, and relies on speed of execution. It has to be able to start a crisis and then back out if it turns out to be too difficult.

Chinese strategy is based on extraordinarily long-term, often multigenerational thinking. For example, the nine-dash line implying that all the South China Sea was Chinese territory began as an eleven-dash line under the predecessor to the communist government. In 1948, the Republic of China (the predecessors to the communists and their mortal opponents in a civil war) issued a diplomatic map that seemed to imply but did not make clear that all the South China Sea was Chinese territory. Thus, even in defeat, the Nationalist government continued to uphold expansionist thinking.

The newly established communist Chinese dictatorship built on the original Nationalist Chinese claims. The South China Sea carries an estimated 11 billion barrels of oil, 190 trillion cubic feet of natural gas, and many of the busiest and wealthiest shipping lanes in the world. It is filled with many small islands, sand bars, and undersea mounts coming to within a few feet of the surface.

Beginning in 2012, the Chinese communists began building bases in the South China Sea. In phase one, the bases are supposed to be peaceful although they already have stands for more than seventy-five military aircraft. The communists have also developed a "fishing" industry that has many more boats than could possibly work in that sea. It is clearly cover for a large semi-military force that can flood any confrontation and force the United States and its allies into sinking civilian ships and causing a public relations disaster.

This pattern of setting big goals, lying about them, then gradually moving step by step to improve China's position while making it more difficult for America and its allies to survive is appearing all over the world. The amazing thing is that this steady, slow aggression is continuing in parallel in an amazing number of places. Simply list all the ports China now has a management contract for and you will be staggered by their penetration of the world commercial system. China also has the largest number of port dredging operations in the world. Similarly, China has been crowding India since 1962 in a series of small border skirmishes.

China is building more roads into the Indian-Chinese mountain boundaries (the highest in the world) and is gradually developing logistic systems that will allow it to dominate in any fight in the mountains.

On a nongeographic basis China has been methodical in its approach to other competitive areas. Chinese activities in space when coupled with the Russians are going to push the Americans harder than any time since the earliest days of the Apollo program. This is also happening with 5G technology, quantum mechanics, and quantum computing. The Chinese potential in biological warfare has been painfully demonstrated over the last two years.

Russia's "hybrid warfare" and China's "asymmetric warfare" pose deep problems for the American system. Neither fits in with Weigley's aforementioned description of the "American way of war." The systems, doctrines, and habits that have made America the dominant military power for a century have now been eclipsed by new thinking, technologies, and systems. The heart of the developing crisis in American survival is the degree to which the American system draws an impossible distinction between "defense" and "national security." The American model has clear divisions between war and peace. Americans make a clear distinction between activities short of war and activities that create a spectrum of violence. Neither Russian hybrid warfare nor Chinese asymmetric warfare fits into our models. Unless we solve this mismatch, we could find ourselves defeated catastrophically.

There are six major zones of potentially catastrophic American defeat:

First is the scale of technological change. There are increasingly competitive systems using increasingly sophisticated science and technology. There are new inventive teams ranging from the big players (Russia and China) to medium-level regimes (North Korea, Iran, Pakistan, Israel, and India) to individual entrepreneurs and companies with start-up focus, drive, and energy and little bureaucracy to slow them down.

Second, we face a huge challenge with the bureaucratic crisis of procurement in speed, cost, and military rather than lobbying criteria. It is the nature of bureaucracies to grow bigger and slower and ultimately worry more about their own existence than the existence of the systems they were set up to serve. We have had radical breakthroughs in communications and information technology. The Pentagon opened in 1943 for staff of 26,000 using manual typewriters and carbon paper to coordinate a global war. The staffing levels haven't changed.[11] Given all the breakthroughs in modern technology, the workforce should be reduced to a triangle and the surplus two-thirds of the building should become a museum of national security.

The current system, which has too many people creating make-work to prove they should be employed, can't possibly keep up with the modern rate of change. This problem is compounded by the number of lobbyists, think tanks, and congressional staffs who further inflate the system with people who have to look important even if they are doing nothing.

Third, we have a crisis of doctrine, from tactics to grand national strategy. No amount of money can replace sound professional doctrine tested against the cauldron of battle. American doctrine for insurgencies has been failing since Vietnam. We have no doctrine that integrates national security, elements of military power, and key elements of national power into a system that can cope with hybrid warfare, asymmetric warfare, insurgencies, and traditional military competition at once. As shocking as it may seem, our enemies are simply better prepared to think about the art of war than we are.

Fourth, we need a dramatic improvement in the nonmilitary sources of national power. To take just one example, in 1983 the Reagan administration issued a report called *A Nation at Risk*.[12] The report was a scathing critique of all the ways public schools were collapsing and failing to teach children. Early on, it said: "If an unfriendly foreign power had attempted to impose on America the mediocre educational performance that exists today, we might well have viewed it as an act of war. As it stands, we have allowed this to happen to ourselves. We have even squandered the gains in student achievement made in the wake of the Sputnik challenge. Moreover, we have dismantled essential support systems which helped make those gains possible. We have, in effect, been committing an act of unthinking, unilateral educational disarmament." The Chinese long-term approach to asymmetric warfare especially challenges us to think through all the elements of national power and come to understand that we have to win at all of them to remain free and safe.

Fifth, we are no closer to defeating radical Islamist threats today than we were in 1996. It is hard to date precisely when the war between radical Islamists and Americans became serious. However, Osama bin Laden dated the war from 1996. Today, there are more radical Islamists than ever before. In countries such as France, they are bolder than ever before. The number of new radical Islamist recruits across the planet almost certainly exceeds the number of radical Islamists who are killed annually. With all the years of Israeli and Western experience, we are still nowhere in finding a useful effective doctrine for defeating the radicals.

Sixth, the newest and most urgent danger to our defense system is the emergence of a cultural civil war inside the Pentagon. One side is there to protect and promote the established bureaucracies and systems. The other side is there to protect and promote the future of America. This could lead to a catastrophe comparable to the collapse of the French army in the 1930s.

The ultimate test will be if the American people, our national security professionals, and our political leadership can force effective reform before we are defeated.

YOU REALLY AIN'T SEEN NOTHING YET

E arlier in this book, I cited President Ronald Reagan's constant use of "you ain't seen nothing yet" to express his optimistic faith in a better American future.

I want to close *Beyond Biden* with the strongest current example of the American commitment to achieving an optimistic, prosperous, free, and safe future. That is the American leadership in space.

Historians will look back on the summer of 2021 as the moment free, entrepreneurial, risk-taking characters broke past the great, dull, boring bureaucracies and reminded people why America *is* an exceptional nation—made up of exceptional people (many of whom migrated here precisely for the freedom to fail and the opportunity to succeed).

In early July, Richard Branson took a six-person crew to the edge of space on a Virgin Galactic vehicle. It was the beginning of his commercial tourism program, which already has 600 people holding reservations.

A few days later, Jeff Bezos flew his brother and an eighty-two-year-old woman into space on a Blue Origin "New Glenn" rocket. This is a wonderfully American moment because Wally Funk was one of the thirteen women who qualified as astronauts in the original program but were rejected because they were told women couldn't succeed in space. She is about to vindicate America's faith in the potential of every American. She is five years older than John Glenn when he went back into space. As the oldest American astronaut, she will be an inspiration both for senior citizens and for women. At the same time, Bezos's brother became the youngest person to fly in space to date.

In September, SpaceX (up to now clearly the most successful entrepreneurial space company) will begin launching passengers into space. Elon Musk has created several industries (PayPal, Tesla, batteries, the Boring Company, commercial space) and is so young, who knows what his next venture will be. Both he and Bezos want to colonize both the moon and Mars—and I wouldn't bet against them.

Finally, a big part of "you really ain't seen nothing yet" is the American willingness to absorb talent.

Branson is from Britain. Musk is from South Africa. Bezos is from Albuquerque, New Mexico (a state that may presently surpass Florida as a center of human space activities).

So be of good cheer.

The future of space flight is just one area in which Americans will lead, take risks, and succeed. In the end, the bad guys will lose, and the exceptional Americans will win again.

ACKNOWLEDGMENTS

Beyond Biden has been challenging and rewarding to write. Over the past two years, our country has gone through a period of transition and dramatic change. The COVID-19 pandemic has transformed how we work, live, and spend time with our loved ones.

Writing this book would not have been possible without the research, analysis, and support of my team—and many others who I have worked with and trusted for years.

My wife, Callista, has been indispensable as the chief executive officer of Gingrich 360. Her spirit, passion, and experience as ambassador to the Holy See have been invaluable and inspiring to our team.

Thanks to my daughters, Kathy Lubbers and Jackie Cushman, who have loved and supported me. Kathy has been an excellent book agent, and Jackie's insights about our country have been incredibly helpful.

The team at Gingrich 360 has worked hard to make this book cohesive and impactful. I would like to thank Louie Brogdon, who coordinated this project. Thanks to Claire Christensen for incorporating her expertise on foreign relations and Joe DeSantis for his longtime advice on health care. I'd like to also thank Rachel Peterson and Aaron Kliegman for their research.

Thanks to Bess Kelly for coordinating our team's efforts. And thanks to Woody Hales for managing my many commitments, Taylor Swindle for managing our finances, and Debbie Myers for her leadership and support.

Additionally, thanks to Garnsey Sloan, producer of my podcast, *Newt's World*. Our Gingrich 360 Network includes Lisa Boothe, Gianno Caldwell, David Grasso, Anna Paulina Luna, C. J. Pearson, Rob Smith, and producer Robert Barowski. The network has greatly contributed to Gingrich 360 by expanding our reach.

Thanks to Allen Silkin and Reid Brown for managing the Gingrich 360 website and social media, and our heroic interns Margaret Smith, Jessica Jacobs, Stetson Bryson, McKenna Daley, Matthew Masino, Isabel McMahon, and Colin Sheffer for their support.

Other major contributors to *Beyond Biden* include the team working on the American Majority Project, which aims to understand the demographics of the nation and prove that conservative values and priorities are supported by a majority of Americans. Joe Gaylord, who helped me design the Contract with America in 1994, is an essential part of this project. His genius is unparalleled and greatly appreciated.

I'd also like to thank John McLaughlin, Stuart Polk, and Brian Larkin at McLaughlin & Associates, who coordinate and execute our polling for the American Majority Project.

Finally, I would like to thank our publisher, Daisy Hutton, and our editor, Alex Pappas, at Hachette Book Group, who worked tirelessly on this project.

I have a phenomenal team, and without them *Beyond Biden* would not have been possible.

ACKNOWLEDGMENTS

ABOUT THE AUTHOR

NEWT GINGRICH is a former Speaker of the U.S. House of Representatives and 2012 presidential candidate. He is chairman of Gingrich 360, a multimedia production and consulting company based in Arlington, Virginia. He is also a Fox News contributor and author of forty-one books, including *New York Times* best sellers *Understanding Trump*, *Trump's America*, *Trump vs. China*, and *Trump and the American Future*. He lives in McLean, Virginia, with his wife, Callista L. Gingrich, former U.S. ambassador to the Holy See.

APPENDIX

NATIONAL SURVEY
RESULTS

McLaughlin & Associates

NATIONAL GINGRICH 360 TOPLINE
GENERAL ELECTION VOTERS: N=1000
MAY 18, 2021

1. WHEN THERE IS A GENERAL ELECTION FOR U.S. SENATE AND CONGRESS, DO YOU ALWAYS VOTE, ALMOST ALWAYS VOTE, VOTE MOST OF THE TIME, HARDLY EVER VOTE, OR NEVER VOTE?

Total	1000
ALWAYS/ALMOST ALWAYS	**88.9**
Always Vote	.64.1
Almost Always Vote	24.7
VOTE MOST OF THE TIME	**11.1**
Mean	**2.53**

2. FOR WHOM DID YOU VOTE IN THE PRESIDENTIAL ELECTION?

Total	1000
DONALD TRUMP	**46.9**
JOE BIDEN	**51.2**
JO JORGENSON	**0.8**
HOWIE HAWKINS	**0.4**
OTHER	**0.2**
DID NOT VOTE/PRESIDENT	**0.2**
DID NOT VOTE AT ALL	**0.3**
DK/REFUSED	**0.0**
Net Diff.	**-4.3**

233

3. **GENERALLY SPEAKING, WOULD YOU SAY THINGS IN THE UNITED STATES ARE GOING IN THE RIGHT DIRECTION, OR HAVE THEY GOTTEN OFF ON THE WRONG TRACK?**

Total	1000
RIGHT DIRECTION	49.3
WRONG TRACK	45.9
DON'T KNOW	4.8
Net Diff.	3.4

4. **IF THE ELECTION FOR U.S. CONGRESS IN YOUR DISTRICT WERE HELD TODAY, WOULD YOU BE MORE LIKELY TO VOTE FOR THE REPUBLICAN CANDIDATE OR THE DEMOCRATIC CANDIDATE?**

Total	1000
REPUBLICAN CANDIDATE	46.7
Definitely	30.1
Probably	9.6
Lean	7.0
DEMOCRATIC CANDIDATE	45.8
Definitely	31.0
Probably	9.0
Lean	5.8
UNDECIDED	7.5
Net Diff.	0.9
Mean	4.00

5. DO YOU APPROVE OR DISAPPROVE OF THE JOB JOE BIDEN IS DOING AS PRESIDENT OF THE UNITED STATES?

Total	1000
APPROVE	**55.7**
Strongly	32.4
Somewhat	23.3
DISAPPROVE	**43.0**
Somewhat	10.0
Strongly	33.0
DON'T KNOW	**1.3**
Net Diff.	**12.7**
Mean	**2.56**

6. DO YOU HAVE A FAVORABLE OR UNFAVORABLE OPINION OF EACH PERSON?

NANCY PELOSI

Total	1000
FAVORABLE	**37.0**
Very	16.6
Somewhat	20.4
UNFAVORABLE	**56.7**
Somewhat	12.1
Very	44.6
NO OPINION	**5.2**
NEVER HEARD OF	**1.1**
Net Diff	**-19.7**
Mean	**2.52**

APPENDIX

7. **NOW, FROM THE FOLLOWING LIST, WHICH ISSUE IS PERSONALLY MOST IMPORTANT TO YOU?**

Total	1000
ECONOMIC	**27.1**
Reopening the Economy	14.5
Create Jobs	8.1
Reduce Gov't Waste	4.5
SOCIAL	**23.6**
Affordable Healthcare	7.0
Reduce Climate Change	5.4
Improve Race Relations	4.1
Protect Medicare	3.7
Improving Education	3.4
SECURITY	**19.7**
Fix Immigration/Border	11.7
Nat'l Sec./Terrorism	4.6
Fight Crime	3.3
CORONAVIRUS	**16.1**
Stop Spread	11.3
Distribute Vaccine	4.7
HONESTY/INTEGRITY/D.C.	**10.9**
DK/REFUSED	**2.7**

8. **DO YOU PRIMARILY THINK OF YOURSELF AN AMERICAN OR A PERSON OF COLOR?**

Total	1000
AMERICAN	**87.2**
PERSON OF COLOR	**8.3**
DON'T KNOW	**4.5**
Net Diff.	**78.9**

9. DO YOU IDENTIFY YOURSELF MORE AS AN AMERICAN, OR BY YOUR RACIAL OR ETHNIC BACKGROUND?

Total	1000
AMERICAN	82.7
RACE/ETHNICITY	13.8
DON'T KNOW	3.5
Net Diff.	68.9

10. DO YOU THINK YOUR FRIENDS AND NEIGHBORS IDENTIFY THEMSELVES MORE AS AMERICANS, OR MORE BY THEIR RACIAL OR ETHNIC BACKGROUNDS?

Total	1000
AMERICAN	75.7
RACE/ETHNICITY	14.1
DON'T KNOW	10.2
Net Diff.	61.6

11. WHEN COMPLETING THE FEDERAL GOVERNMENT CENSUS OF LAST YEAR, HOW WOULD YOU HAVE DESCRIBED YOUR RACIAL BACKGROUND?

Total	1000
WHITE/CAUCASIAN	70.8
BLACK/AFRICAN AMERICAN	13.8
HISPANIC/LATINO/SPANISH	7.5
AM. INDIAN/AK NATIVE	0.6
ASIAN/PACIFIC ISLANDER	3.8
OTHER	0.7
MIXED RACE	2.3
DON'T KNOW/REFUSED	0.6

12. **ARE YOU, YOUR PARENTS OR GRANDPARENTS OR SOMEONE IN YOUR IMMEDIATE HOUSEHOLD AN IMMIGRANT TO THE UNITED STATES?**

Total	1000
YES	**39.9**
Immigrated/USA	8.9
Parents/Immigrants	6.6
Grandparents/Immigrants	19.1
Immediate Household	2.5
More Than One of Above	2.8
NONE	**57.5**
DK/REFUSED	**2.7**

13. **PLEASE INDICATE WHETHER YOU AGREE OR DISAGREE WITH EACH OF THE FOLLOWING STATEMENTS**

   THE UNITED STATES OF AMERICA IS THE GREATEST COUNTRY ON EARTH.

Total	1000
AGREE	**78.1**
Strongly	48.6
Somewhat	29.5
DISAGREE	**18.6**
Somewhat	11.2
Strongly	7.4
DON'T KNOW	**3.3**
Net Diff.	**59.4**
Mean	**3.23**

14. **THE UNITED STATES OF AMERICA IS THE MOST FREE AND DEMOCRATIC COUNTRY IN THE WORLD.**

Total	1000
AGREE	**74.9**
Strongly	.41.9
Somewhat	33.0
DISAGREE	**21.3**
Somewhat	14.5
Strongly	6.8
DON'T KNOW	**3.8**
Net Diff.	**53.6**
Mean	**.3.14**

15. **THE UNITED STATES OF AMERICA IS LIVING UP TO ITS FOUNDING IDEALS OF FREEDOM, EQUALITY AND SELF GOVERNANCE.**

Total	1000
AGREE	**48.4**
Strongly	19.2
Somewhat	29.2
DISAGREE	**48.0**
Somewhat	29.2
Strongly	18.8
DON'T KNOW	**3.6**
Net Diff.	**0.4**
Mean	**2.51**

16. THE UNITED STATES IS SYSTEMICALLY RACIST.

Total	1000
AGREE	**48.8**
Strongly	20.2
Somewhat	28.6
DISAGREE	**46.1**
Somewhat	17.5
Strongly	28.6
DON'T KNOW	**5.1**
Net Diff.	**2.7**
Mean	**2.43**

17. WITH DR. MARTIN LUTHER KING THAT THE CONTENT OF A PERSON'S CHARACTER IS MORE IMPORTANT THAN THE COLOR OF THEIR SKIN.

Total	1000
AGREE	**91.2**
Strongly	72.3
Somewhat	18.9
DISAGREE	**5.4**
Somewhat	2.9
Strongly	2.5
DON'T KNOW	**3.4**
Net Diff.	**85.9**
Mean	**3.67**

18. DO YOU APPROVE OR DISAPPROVE OF REQUIRING NEEDY ABLE-BODIED ADULTS TO WORK FOR TAXPAYER FUNDED BENEFITS SUCH AS FOOD STAMPS, HEALTHCARE OR WELFARE?

Total	1000
APPROVE	**74.3**
Strongly	.41.4
Somewhat	32.9
DISAPPROVE	**16.2**
Somewhat	9.9
Strongly	6.2
DON'T KNOW	**9.5**
Net Diff.	**58.2**
Mean	**3.21**

19. WHICH IS THE MORE IMPORTANT FEDERAL POLICY?

1. TAKING CARE OF PEOPLE WHO ARE IN NEED EVEN THOUGH THEY MAY BECOME DEPENDENT ON GOVERNMENT

2. ENCOURAGING PEOPLE WHO ARE IN NEED TO WORK AND BE LESS DEPENDENT UPON GOVERNMENT ASSISTANCE

Total	1000
TAKE CARE OF PEOPLE	**32.6**
ENCOURAGE LESS DPDNCE	**59.0**
DON'T KNOW	**8.4**
Net Diff.	**26.4**

20. DO YOU APPROVE OR DISAPPROVE OF PRESIDENT BIDEN'S RECENT EXECUTIVE ORDER ELIMINATING WORK REQUIREMENTS FOR ABLE-BODIED ADULTS IN NEED TO RECEIVE GOVERNMENT ASSISTANCE?

Total	1000
APPROVE	**40.4**
Strongly	18.1
Somewhat	22.3
DISAPPROVE	**49.4**
Somewhat	18.2
Strongly	31.2
DON'T KNOW	**10.2**
Net Diff.	**-9.0**
Mean	**2.30**

21. FROM THE FOLLOWING LIST, WHAT SOCIAL NETWORKS DO YOU USE?

Total	1000
FACEBOOK	**76.8**
YOUTUBE	**64.0**
INSTAGRAM	**41.7**
TWITTER	**30.6**
PINTEREST	**30.4**
LINKED-IN	**22.2**
SNAPCHAT	**19.2**
TIKTOK	**19.1**
REDDIT	**15.0**
WHATSAPP	**15.0**
TUMBLR	**7.8**
TELEGRAM	**5.2**

PARLER 4.6
GAB.COM 2.9
RUMBLE 2.6
CLOUTHUB 1.3
OTHER 0.3
NONE 5.7

22. THINKING ABOUT A POLITICAL PARTY, WOULD YOU CONSIDER
    YOURSELF A . . . ?

Total	1000
REPUBLICAN	36.0
DEMOCRAT.	37.0
INDEPENDENT/OTHER	27.0
Net Diff.	-1.0

23. IF YOU WERE TO LABEL YOURSELF, WOULD YOU SAY YOU ARE A
    LIBERAL, A MODERATE, OR A CONSERVATIVE IN YOUR POLITICAL
    BELIEFS?

Total	1000
LIBERAL	29.7
Very.	.17.2
Somewhat.	12.5
MODERATE.	33.2
CONSERVATIVE	.37.1
Somewhat.	18.6
Very.	18.5
DK/REFUSED	0.0
Net Diff.	.7.4
Mean.	3.09

24. WHICH OF THE FOLLOWING BEST DESCRIBES YOUR RELIGION/ RELIGIOUS AFFILIATION/IDENTIFICATION?

Total	1000
PROTESTANT	38.4
ROMAN CATHOLIC	22.9
AGNOSTIC	6.1
ATHEIST	3.3
JEWISH	3.1
BUDDHIST	1.7
MUSLIM	1.6
MORMON	1.5
HINDU	0.7
SECULAR	0.6
EASTERN/GREEK	0.6
SIKH	0.1
OTHER	2.8
NONE	16.5

25. DO YOU CONSIDER YOURSELF AN EVANGELICAL OR BORN-AGAIN CHRISTIAN?

Total Answering	613
YES	46.8
NO	53.2
Net Diff.	-6.3

26. WHAT IS CURRENTLY YOUR MARITAL STATUS?

Total	1000
SINGLE	37.6
Never Married................	28.9
Live w/Sig. Other	8.7
MARRIED......................	43.0
SEPARATED	1.5
DIVORCED.....................	11.8
WIDOWED	6.2

27. HOW WOULD YOU DESCRIBE YOUR PRESENT EMPLOYMENT SITUATION – A JOB IN THE PRIVATE SECTOR, A JOB WITH THE GOVERNMENT, SELF-EMPLOYED, HOMEMAKER, STUDENT, RETIRED OR NOT EMPLOYED?

Total	1000
EMPLOYED	46.2
Private Sector................	39.3
Government	6.8
SELF EMPLOYED	9.2
HOMEMAKER	6.4
STUDENT......................	4.1
RETIRED	24.7
NOT EMPLOYED................	9.4

28. WHAT IS YOUR ANNUAL HOUSEHOLD INCOME?

Total	1000
UNDER $20k	14.8
$20-$40k	23.1
$40-$60k	20.1
$60-$100k	22.6
$100-$150k	11.5
$150-$200k	4.9
$200-$250k	1.4
OVER $250k	1.5
Mean	68056.33

29. WOULD YOU CONSIDER WHERE YOU LIVE TO BE A URBAN, SUBURBAN OR RURAL AREA?

Total	1000
URBAN AREA	31.3
SUBURBAN AREA	49.6
RURAL AREA	19.2

30. WOULD YOU CONSIDER YOURSELF . . . ?

Total	1000
WEALTHY	4.7
MIDDLE CLASS	86.4
Upper Middle Class	10.5
Middle Class	49.2
Lower Middle Class	26.7
POOR	8.9
Mean	2.75

31. ARE YOU OR IS A MEMBER OF YOUR IMMEDIATE FAMILY FROM A LATINO, HISPANIC OR SPANISH SPEAKING BACKGROUND?

Total	1000
YES	13.3
NO	86.7

32. WHAT IS YOUR MAIN RACIAL BACKGROUND?

Total	1000
HISPANIC	13.3
AFRICAN AMERICAN	13.3
ASIAN	4.0
WHITE	.67.7
OTHER	1.7

33. WHAT IS YOUR AGE? ARE YOU BETWEEN . . .

Total	1000
18-29	.17.2
30-40	15.8
41-55	25.0
56-65	19.9
OVER 65	22.1
Mean	49.19

34. GENDER:

Total	1000
MALE	48.0
FEMALE	52.0

35. REGION:

Total	1000
NEW ENGLAND	5.2
MIDDLE ATLANTIC	13.0
EAST NORTH CENTRAL	15.7
WEST NORTH CENTRAL	6.8
SOUTH ATLANTIC	21.7
EAST SOUTH CENTRAL	5.6
WEST SOUTH CENTRAL	10.1
MOUNTAIN	7.5
PACIFIC	14.4

36. AREA:

Total	1000
EAST	18.2
MIDWEST	22.5
SOUTH	37.4
WEST	21.9

NATIONAL SURVEY ANALYSIS
MARCH 2021
Presented by McLaughlin & Asociates

METHODOLOGY

This national survey was conducted among 1,000 likely general election voters with an oversample of 238 Republican likely voters. Combined, there is a total sample of 600 Republican voters. The Republican voter oversample has been weighted proportionately into the 1,000 likely voter national sample. All interviews were conducted between January 29 and February 2, 2021.

All interviews were conducted online and survey invitations were distributed randomly within predetermined geographic units. These units were structured to correlate with actual voter turnout nationwide in a general election.

The sample of 1,000 likely general election voters has an accuracy of +/- 3.1% at a 95% confidence interval. The sample of 600 Republican likely voters has an accuracy of +/- 4.0% at a 95% confidence interval. The numbers in this presentation have been rounded and may not equal 100%.

MAJOR FINDINGS

- Partisan Parity

- Conservative Plurality

- The nation and congress are on the wrong track.

- Joe Biden is on a honeymoon.

- The congressional vote and impeachment are polarizing the country by partisanship.

- Republicans don't trust their Party's leadership, which can split their Party.

- President Trump is still the dominant Republican leader and the majority of Republicans want him to run again.

- Developing a strong popular agenda is the way to unite and broaden the Republican Party to win back congress and the presidency.

PARTY AFFILIATION

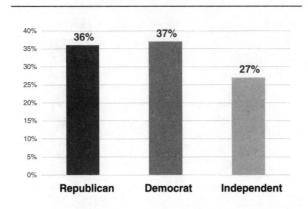

	GOP	DEM	IND	Net
TOTAL	36	37	27	-1
Voted Trump	67	7	26	60
Voted Biden	9	65	26	-56
Approve Trump	61	15	24	46
Disapprove Trump	11	59	30	-48
Approve Biden	17	57	26	-40
Disapprove Biden	66	6	28	60
Vote Republican	73	8	19	65
Vote Democrat	4	74	22	-70
Undecided	16	9	75	7
Liberal	11	75	14	-64
Moderate	18	39	43	-21
Conservative	70	10	19	60
White	43	28	29	15
Black	8	71	21	-63
Hispanic	30	55	15	-25
18-40	25	54	22	-29
41-55	28	37	36	-9
56+	49	25	26	24
Men	40	35	26	5
Women	33	40	28	-7
Urban	24	50	26	-26
Suburban	39	35	26	4
Rural	46	24	30	22

IDEOLOGY

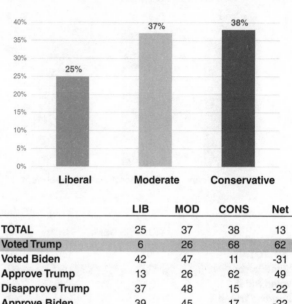

	LIB	MOD	CONS	Net
TOTAL	25	37	38	13
Voted Trump	6	26	68	62
Voted Biden	42	47	11	-31
Approve Trump	13	26	62	49
Disapprove Trump	37	48	15	-22
Approve Biden	39	45	17	-22
Disapprove Biden	3	25	72	69
Vote Republican	8	21	71	63
Vote Democrat	46	45	9	-37
Undecided	8	66	26	18
Republican	8	18	74	66
Democrat	50	39	11	-39
Independent	13	59	28	15
Ind. Men	12	59	29	17
Ind. Women	14	60	26	12
White	21	34	45	24
Black	40	49	12	-28
Hispanic	36	37	27	-9
18-40	40	41	20	-20
41-55	23	44	33	10
56+	15	30	54	39
Men	25	34	42	17
Women	25	41	35	10
Urban	36	38	26	-10
Suburban	21	38	41	20
Rural	19	32	50	31

DIRECTION: UNITED STATES

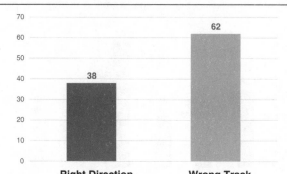

	Right	Wrong	Net
TOTAL	38	62	-24
Voted Trump	18	81	-63
Voted Biden	56	45	11
Approve Trump	26	74	-48
Disapprove Trump	49	51	-2
Approve Biden	56	44	12
Disapprove Biden	8	91	-83
Vote Republican	21	79	-58
Vote Democrat	58	42	16
Undecided	22	78	-56
Liberal	62	38	24
Moderate	41	59	-18
Conservative	18	82	-64
Republican	21	79	-58
Democrat	60	40	20
Independent	29	70	-41
Ind. Men	27	73	-46
Ind. Women	32	68	-36
Non-College Grad.	37	63	-26
College Grad	38	62	-24
White	31	69	-38
Black	62	39	23
Hispanic	48	51	-3
18-40	55	45	10
41-55	39	61	-22
56+	24	76	-52
Men	37	63	-26
Women	38	62	-24
Urban	50	50	0
Suburban	36	64	-28
Rural	24	76	-52

JOB RATING: CONGRESS

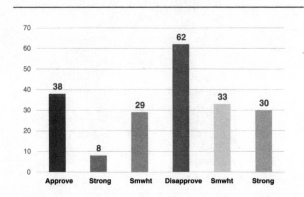

	Approve	Disapprove	Net
TOTAL	38	62	-24
Voted Trump	22	79	-57
Voted Biden	53	47	6
Approve Trump	30	70	-40
Disapprove Trump	46	54	-8
Approve Biden	54	46	8
Disapprove Biden	13	87	-74
Vote Republican	24	76	-52
Vote Democrat	55	44	11
Undecided	22	78	-56
Liberal	63	37	26
Moderate	36	64	-28
Conservative	22	77	-55
Republican	26	74	-48
Democrat	59	41	18
Independent	24	75	-51
Ind. Men	19	81	-62
Ind. Women	29	70	-41
Non-College Grad.	39	61	-22
College Grad	36	64	-28
White	31	69	-38
Black	58	42	16
Hispanic	52	48	4
18-40	54	46	8
41-55	42	58	-16
56+	24	76	-52
Men	35	65	-30
Women	40	60	-20
Urban	49	51	-2
Suburban	34	66	-32
Rural	30	70	-40

IMAGE: MITCH MCCONNELL

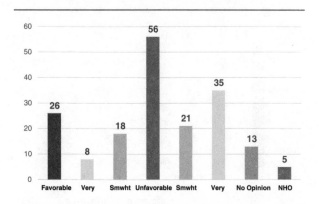

	Favorable	Unfavorable	Net
TOTAL	26	56	-30
Voted Trump	39	44	-5
Voted Biden	14	68	-54
Approve Trump	42	42	0
Disapprove Trump	11	70	-59
Approve Biden	19	63	-44
Disapprove Biden	37	46	-9
Vote Republican	40	46	-6
Vote Democrat	15	70	-55
Undecided	17	43	-26
Liberal	19	66	-47
Moderate	16	60	-44
Conservative	40	47	-7
Republican	41	46	-5
Democrat	18	66	-48
Independent	17	57	-40
Ind. Men	18	65	-47
Ind. Women	17	49	-32
Non-College Grad.	21	56	-35
College Grad	33	56	-23
White	30	56	-26
Black	13	56	-43
Hispanic	23	55	-32
18-40	25	49	-24
41-55	20	59	-39
56+	31	60	-29
Men	32	57	-25
Women	20	56	-36
Urban	25	56	-31
Suburban	28	56	-28
Rural	24	58	-34

IMAGE: KEVIN MCCARTHY

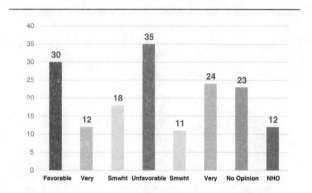

	Favorable	Unfavorable	Net
TOTAL	30	35	-5
Voted Trump	44	18	26
Voted Biden	17	51	-34
Approve Trump	47	18	29
Disapprove Trump	12	52	-40
Approve Biden	20	45	-25
Disapprove Biden	45	20	25
Vote Republican	46	20	26
Vote Democrat	18	53	-35
Undecided	12	24	-12
Liberal	22	47	-25
Moderate	17	43	-26
Conservative	47	20	27
Republican	44	23	21
Democrat	21	46	-25
Independent	22	36	-14
Ind. Men	27	43	-16
Ind. Women	18	29	-11
Non-College Grad.	25	33	-8
College Grad	36	38	-2
White	32	34	-2
Black	16	42	-26
Hispanic	30	33	-3
18-40	27	28	-1
41-55	25	37	-12
56+	34	39	-5
Men	37	40	-3
Women	21	30	-9
Urban	34	34	0
Suburban	29	36	-7
Rural	26	34	-8

JOB RATING: JOE BIDEN

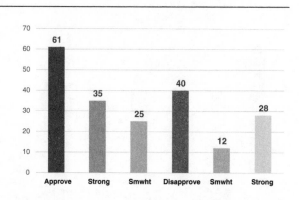

	Approve	Disapprove	Net
TOTAL	61	40	21
Voted Trump	21	79	-58
Voted Biden	97	3	94
Approve Trump	30	71	-41
Disapprove Trump	91	9	82
Approve Biden	100	0	100
Disapprove Biden	0	100	-100
Vote Republican	26	74	-48
Vote Democrat	97	3	94
Undecided	54	46	8
Liberal	95	5	90
Moderate	73	27	46
Conservative	26	74	-48
Republican	29	71	-42
Democrat	93	7	86
Independent	58	42	16
Ind. Men	58	42	16
Ind. Women	59	41	18
Non-College Grad.	59	41	18
College Grad	63	37	26
White	53	47	6
Black	89	11	78
Hispanic	71	29	42
18-40	75	25	50
41-55	64	36	28
56+	48	52	-4
Men	60	40	20
Women	61	39	22
Urban	77	23	54
Suburban	58	42	16
Rural	43	57	-14

JOB RATING: JOE BIDEN

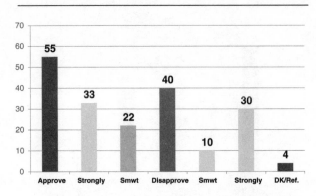

	Approve	Disapprove
East	64	34
Midwest	55	40
South	53	42
West	53	42
Vote Trump 2020	18	78
Vote Biden 2020	90	7
Vote Cong. – GOP	23	73
Vote Cong. – DEM	90	8
Vote Cong.– UND	46	40
Approve Biden	100	0
Disapprove Biden	0	100
Republican	26	70
Democrat	90	8
Independent	48	45
Liberal	88	10
Moderate	64	30
Conservative	22	74
White	45	51
African- American	88	10
Hispanic	74	23
Under 55	67	28
Over 55	39	57
Married	49	46
Single	71	26
Men	51	45
Women	59	36
Live in Urban Area	71	24
Live in Suburban Area	53	44
Live in Rural Area	40	54

If Donald Trump won the Republican nomination for President, would you vote for him in the 2024 general election? (Republican Primary Voters)

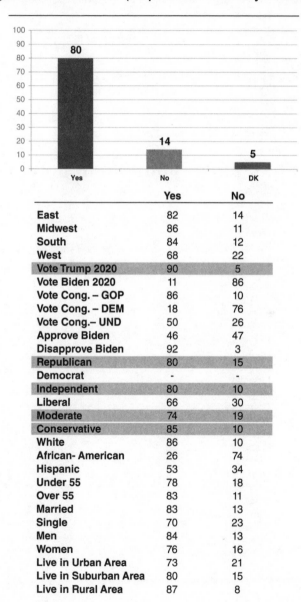

	Yes	No
East	82	14
Midwest	86	11
South	84	12
West	68	22
Vote Trump 2020	90	5
Vote Biden 2020	11	86
Vote Cong. – GOP	86	10
Vote Cong. – DEM	18	76
Vote Cong.– UND	50	26
Approve Biden	46	47
Disapprove Biden	92	3
Republican	80	15
Democrat	-	-
Independent	80	10
Liberal	66	30
Moderate	74	19
Conservative	85	10
White	86	10
African- American	26	74
Hispanic	53	34
Under 55	78	18
Over 55	83	11
Married	83	13
Single	70	23
Men	84	13
Women	76	16
Live in Urban Area	73	21
Live in Suburban Area	80	15
Live in Rural Area	87	8

GENERIC BALLOT: U.S. CONGRESS
Time Series

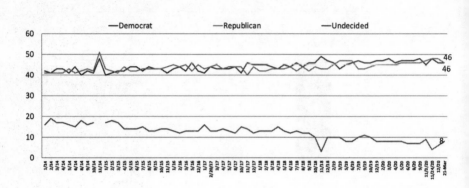

Thinking ahead to the 2024 Republican primary election for president, if that election were held today among the following candidates, for whom would you vote? (Republican Primary Voters)

	11/20 (N=442)	12/20 (N=438)	3/21 (N=448)
Donald Trump, JR	20	20	21
Mike Pence	30	20	15
Ted Cruz	5	7	9
Ron DeSantis	2	2	9
Mitt Romney	5	5	6
Nikki Haley	8	6	5
Candace Owens	*	*	4
Ivanka Trump	*	4	3
John Kasich	2	3	2
Marco Rubio	2	3	2
Tom Cotton	1	2	2
Kristi Noem	1	2	2
Tim Scott	1	2	2
Mike Pompeo	*	1	2
Rick Scott	1	0.4	1
Tucker Carlson	2	1	1
Undecided	21	22	17

Thinking ahead to the 2024 Democratic primary election for President, if that election were held today among the following candidates, for whom would you vote? (Democrat Primary Voters)

	11/20 (N=445)	12/20 (N=443)	3/21 (N=443)
Kamala Harris	29	25	28
Michelle Obama	23	29	23
Pete Buttigieg	6	5	7
Alexandria Ocasio-Cortez	6	7	8
Andrew Cuomo	5	5	1
Cory Booker	2	3	4
Amy Klobuchar	2	2	3
John Hickenlooper	1	3	2
Deval Patrick	1	1	1
Kirsten Gillibrand	1	1	1
Tim Kaine	1	2	1
Ilhan Omar	1	1	1
Andrew Yang	*	*	4
Beto O'Rourke	*	*	2
Gavin Newsom	*	*	0
Undecided	23	18	14

JOB RATING
JOE BIDEN DISTRIBUTING THE VACCINE

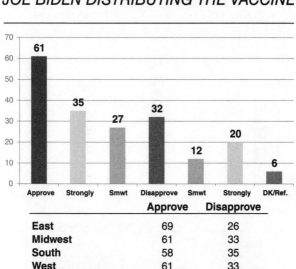

	Approve	Disapprove
East	69	26
Midwest	61	33
South	58	35
West	61	33
Vote Trump 2020	29	60
Vote Biden 2020	90	7
Vote Cong. – GOP	33	58
Vote Cong. – DEM	92	6
Vote Cong.– UND	53	34
Approve Biden	94	4
Disapprove Biden	18	73
Republican	35	55
Democrat	91	7
Independent	56	37
Liberal	85	11
Moderate	70	26
Conservative	35	55
White	55	39
African- American	79	16
Hispanic	79	15
Under 55	71	25
Over 55	49	43
Married	56	38
Single	73	22
Men	59	37
Women	64	28
Live in Urban Area	75	21
Live in Suburban Area	60	36
Live in Rural Area	46	41

OPINION
NANCY PELOSI

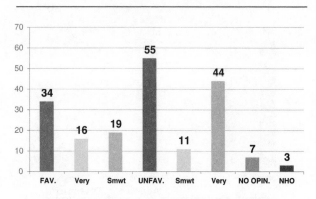

	Favorable	Unfavorable
East	40	51
Midwest	33	59
South	32	56
West	36	54
Vote Trump 2020	9	85
Vote Biden 2020	58	28
Vote Cong. – GOP	12	81
Vote Cong. – DEM	60	28
Vote Cong.– UND	19	67
Approve Biden	59	29
Disapprove Biden	3	92
Republican	12	82
Democrat	62	23
Independent	27	64
Liberal	64	24
Moderate	34	52
Conservative	11	83
White	30	65
African- American	46	26
Hispanic	42	38
Under 55	39	46
Over 55	28	68
Married	31	61
Single	41	41
Men	33	61
Women	36	50
Live in Urban Area	49	39
Live in Suburban Area	31	60
Live in Rural Area	23	68

Do you want to see Donald Trump run for President again in 2024? (Republican Primary Voters)

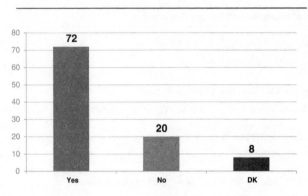

	Yes	No
East	72	19
Midwest	78	16
South	77	17
West	57	31
Vote Trump 2020	79	12
Vote Biden 2020	17	82
Vote Cong. – GOP	76	16
Vote Cong. – DEM	14	82
Vote Cong.– UND	65	26
Approve Biden	43	51
Disapprove Biden	82	9
Republican	71	21
Democrat	-	-
Independent	76	14
Liberal	67	33
Moderate	70	19
Conservative	73	18
White	75	16
African- American	15	85
Hispanic	60	33
Under 55	75	20
Over 55	70	20
Married	73	18
Single	67	30
Men	71	20
Women	74	19
Live in Urban Area	67	25
Live in Suburban Area	69	22
Live in Rural Area	81	13

APPROVALS: TOTAL RANKING (ALL ISSUES)

Approve/Disapprove (Strongly Approve)	Total
Requiring health insurance to cover all pre-existing conditions.	89/11 (61)
Cutting prescription drug prices through consumer choice and private sector competition.	89/11 (56)
Mandatory deportation for non-citizen gang members.	87/13 (63)
Giving a "Made in America" tax credit to businesses who make their products in America.	87/13 (51)
Enacting term limits on members of Congress and the U.S. Senate.	86/14 (58)
Requiring signature verification for any mail-in ballot voting.	85/15 (55)
Protecting religious freedom from government interference.	85/15 (54)
Lowering health insurance premiums through more consumer choice and private sector competition.	85/15 (47)
Allowing only American citizens to vote in elections.	84/16 (64)
Requiring fair trade with communist China to bring back manufacturing jobs from China to America.	82/18 (44)
Requiring photo identification to vote.	81/19 (56)
Allowing school choice for every American child.	81/19 (47)
Passing anti-trust legislation to regulate Big Tech social media companies to protect competition, free speech, and privacy.	81/19 (39)

APPROVALS: TOTAL RANKING (ALL ISSUES)

Approve/Disapprove (Strongly Approve)	Total
Fully fund our police and law enforcement.	80/20 (52)
Requiring the use of masks and social distancing in all federal buildings, on federal lands and by federal employees and contractors.	78/22 (52)
Prioritizing Opportunity Zones for investing in urban areas.	77/23 (26)
Maximizing our oil and gas production to keep America energy independent.	75/25 (49)
Ending giveaways for those here illegally like taxpayer funded welfare, health care, and free college tuition for illegal immigrants.	75/25 (46)
Requiring Big Tech social media companies to guarantee free speech and subject them to the same federal regulations as other media corporations.	75/25 (44)
Cutting federal income taxes.	75/25 (40)
Expanding the child tax credit from $2,000 to $3,000 per child.	75/25 (37)
Requiring mandatory life sentences in prison for cop killers.	74/26 (47)
Reforming immigration laws to encourage people with skills and education to come to America, rather than just basing it on family reunification.	74/26 (33)
Enacting term limits on members of the United States Supreme Court.	73/27 (41)

APPROVALS: TOTAL RANKING (ALL ISSUES)

Approve/Disapprove (Strongly Approve)	Total
Promoting free and democratic elections, and human rights in China.	73/27 (33)
Banning abortions after 20 weeks, or five months of pregnancy, when an unborn child can feel pain.	72/28 (46)
Requiring mandatory prison sentences for anyone who physically attacks the police.	72/28 (42)
Defending Israel from Iran.	69/31 (36)
Suspending the payroll tax to save and create jobs until the economy recovers.	69/31 (33)
Requiring Big Tech companies like Facebook, Google, Apple, Twitter, and Amazon to guarantee free speech for American citizens on their social media platforms.	68/32 (40)
Rolling back government restrictions to return to normal this year.	68/32 (33)
Calling for a federal investigation into allegations of election fraud.	67/33 (40)
Ending cashless bail that allows dangerous criminals to go free while waiting for trial.	66/34 (43)
Restoring pro-family gender language to congress that would end congress' ban on using words like father, mother, son, daughter, brother, sister, husband, and wife.	66/34 (41)
Banning social media scores where Big Tech and government monitor every American citizen's social views and statements like they do in Communist China.	66/34 (41)

APPROVALS: TOTAL RANKING (ALL ISSUES)

Approve/Disapprove (Strongly Approve)	Total
Ending Sanctuary Cities.	64/36 (41)
Appointing conservative Supreme Court Judges.	63/37 (31)
Completing the border wall with Mexico.	57/43 (39)
Mandating a federal ban on taxpayer funded abortions.	56/44 (35)
Providing amnesty and path to citizenship for over 11-million illegal immigrants.	53/47 (21)
Making Washington D.C. and Puerto Rico states, which would add 4 new voting U.S. Senators and as many as 7 new voting members Congress.	51/49 (22)
Increasing taxes to make all public colleges and universities tuition-free.	41/59 (17)
Promoting transgenderism in public schools, starting in elementary school.	40/60 (14)
Expanding the U.S. Supreme Court so one party can get a political advantage.	30/69 (15)

DISAPPROVALS: TOTAL RANKING BY DISAPPROVE

Approve/Disapprove (Strongly Approve)	Total
Expanding the U.S. Supreme Court so one party can get a political advantage.	30/69 (43)
Promoting transgenderism in public schools, starting in elementary school.	40/60 (38)
Increasing taxes to make all public colleges and universities tuition-free.	41/59 (39)

APPROVALS: ELECTIONS

APPROVE/DISAPPROVE (Strongly Approve)

	Total	Voted Trump	GOP	IND	Mod	Cons
Requiring signature verification for any mail-in ballot voting.	85/15 (55)	92/8 (74)	92/8 (70)	84/16 (59)	83/17 (48)	91/9 (75)
Allowing only American citizens to vote in elections.	84/16 (64)	93/7 (81)	93/7 (78)	79/21 (65)	82/18 (56)	95/5 (85)
Requiring photo identification to vote.	81/19 (56)	92/8 (78)	90/10 (74)	80/20 (56)	77/23 (47)	95/5 (80)
Calling for a federal investigation into allegations of election fraud.	67/33 (40)	88/12 (65)	85/15 (61)	58/42 (36)	57/43 (28)	86/14 (64)

APPROVALS: REFORMS, SWAMP & BIG TECH

APPROVE/DISAPPROVE (Strongly Approve)

	Total	Voted Trump	GOP	IND	Mod	Cons
Enacting term limits on members of Congress and the U.S. Senate.	86/14 (58)	91/9 (65)	92/8 (64)	85/15 (61)	83/17 (54)	92/8 (68)
Passing anti-trust legislation to regulate Big Tech social media companies to protect competition, free speech, and privacy.	81/19 (39)	88/12 (53)	87/13 (49)	78/22 (37)	78/22 (28)	88/12 (56)
Requiring Big Tech social media companies to guarantee free speech and subject them to the same federal regulations as other media corporations.	75/25 (44)	88/12 (63)	89/11 (60)	68/32 (39)	69/31 (30)	89/11 (67)
Enacting term limits on members of the United States Supreme Court.	73/27 (41)	70/30 (44)	72/28 (46)	72/28 (38)	77/23 (37)	72/28 (46)
Requiring Big Tech companies like Facebook, Google, Apple, Twitter, and Amazon to guarantee free speech for American citizens on their social media platforms.	68/32 (40)	83/17 (60)	80/20 (56)	69/31 (38)	65/35 (28)	83/17 (62)

(Continued)

APPROVALS: REFORMS, SWAMP & BIG TECH

APPROVE/DISAPPROVE (Strongly Approve)

	Total	Voted Trump	GOP	IND	Mod	Cons
Rolling back government restrictions to return to normal this year.	68/32 (33)	79/21 (46)	77/23 (43)	67/33 (32)	63/37 (26)	79/21 (48)
Banning social media scores where Big Tech and government monitor every American citizen's social views and statements like they do in Communist China.	66/34 (41)	74/26 (58)	73/27 (55)	62/38 (40)	61/39 (30)	74/26 (60)
Expanding the U.S. Supreme Court so one party can get a political advantage.	30/69 (15)	20/79 (10)	24/76 (13)	20/80 (9)	26/73 (12)	18/82 (9)
Making Washington D.C. and Puerto Rico states, which would add 4 new voting U.S. Senators and as many as 7 new voting members Congress.	51/49 (22)	26/74 (8)	29/71 (11)	51/49 (18)	57/43 (20)	28/72 (12)

APPROVALS: IMMIGRATION

APPROVE/DISAPPROVE (Strongly Approve)

	Total	Voted Trump	GOP	IND	Mod	Cons
Mandatory deportation for non-citizen gang members.	87/13 (63)	92/8 (78)	92/8 (76)	86/14 (61)	85/15 (55)	94/6 (80)
Ending giveaways for those here illegally like taxpayer funded welfare, health care, and free college tuition for illegal immigrants.	75/25 (46)	89/11 (69)	90/10 (67)	77/23 (48)	74/26 (35)	86/14 (68)
Reforming immigration laws to encourage people with skills and education to come to America, rather than just basing it on family reunification.	74/26 (33)	74/26 (38)	74/26 (41)	73/27 (28)	72/28 (24)	76/24 (42)
Ending Sanctuary Cities.	64/36 (41)	84/16 (68)	81/19 (65)	65/35 (35)	52/48 (27)	89/11 (71)
Completing the border wall with Mexico.	57/43 (39)	87/13 (69)	81/19 (65)	53/47 (33)	45/55 (23)	86/14 (70)
Providing amnesty and path to citizenship for over 11-million illegal immigrants.	53/47 (21)	32/68 (9)	35/65 (10)	49/51 (17)	57/43 (18)	33/67 (12)

273

APPROVALS: SECURITY & DEFENSE

APPROVE/DISAPPROVE (Strongly Approve)

	Total	Voted Trump	GOP	IND	Mod	Cons
Fully fund our police and law enforcement.	80/20 (52)	90/10 (72)	90/10 (72)	82/18 (51)	80/20 (44)	91/9 (73)
Requiring mandatory life sentences in prison for cop killers.	74/26 (47)	83/17 (57)	86/14 (58)	70/30 (41)	67/33 (39)	88/12 (62)
Requiring mandatory prison sentences for anyone who physically attacks the police.	72/28 (42)	84/16 (58)	86/14 (58)	66/34 (43)	64/36 (34)	89/11 (62)
Defending Israel from Iran.	69/31 (36)	77/23 (52)	79/21 (50)	71/29 (37)	58/42 (23)	80/20 (55)
Ending cashless bail that allows dangerous criminals to go free while waiting for trial.	66/34 (43)	72/28 (55)	75/25 (55)	61/39 (41)	59/41 (35)	74/26 (57)

APPROVALS: ECONOMICS

APPROVE/DISAPPROVE (Strongly Approve)

	Total	Voted Trump	GOP	IND	Mod	Cons
Giving a "Made in America" tax credit to businesses who make their products in America.	87/13 (51)	89/11 (61)	91/8 (59)	83/17 (47)	84/16 (42)	92/8 (64)
Prioritizing Opportunity Zones for investing in urban areas.	77/23 (26)	72/28 (25)	70/30 (22)	74/26 (23)	79/21 (20)	70/30 (25)
Maximizing our oil and gas production to keep America energy independent.	75/25 (49)	90/10 (69)	89/11 (67)	76/24 (47)	72/28 (41)	90/10 (71)
Cutting federal income taxes.	75/25 (40)	83/17 (55)	83/17 (49)	69/31 (42)	73/27 (29)	86/14 (60)
Expanding the child tax credit from $2,000 to $3,000 per child.	75/25 (37)	67/33 (30)	64/36 (29)	75/25 (30)	77/23 (32)	65/35 (33)
Suspending the payroll tax to save and create jobs until the economy recovers.	69/31 (33)	70/30 (36)	67/33 (31)	65/35 (29)	68/32 (29)	70/30 (32)

APPROVALS: SOCIAL ISSUES

APPROVE/DISAPPROVE (Strongly Approve)

	Total	Voted Trump	GOP	IND	Mod	Cons
Requiring health insurance to cover all pre-existing conditions.	89/11 (61)	89/11 (57)	89/11 (60)	88/12 (57)	87/13 (59)	90/10 (60)
Cutting prescription drug prices through consumer choice and private sector competition.	89/11 (56)	93/7 (62)	93/7 (60)	90/10 (57)	89/11 (48)	93/7 (64)
Lowering health insurance premiums through more consumer choice and private sector competition.	85/15 (47)	91/9 (53)	90/10 (53)	84/16 (44)	81/19 (42)	93/7 (56)
Allowing school choice for every American child.	81/19 (47)	87/13 (53)	86/14 (50)	84/16 (50)	79/21 (41)	86/14 (54)
Requiring the use of masks and social distancing in all federal buildings, on federal lands and by federal employees and contractors.	78/22 (52)	69/31 (39)	73/27 (44)	77/23 (53)	83/17 (54)	69/31 (44)
Increasing taxes to make all public colleges and universities tuition-free.	41/59 (17)	19/81 (6)	22/78 (7)	38/62 (15)	46/54 (15)	19/81 (8)

APPROVALS: MORAL ISSUES

APPROVE/DISAPPROVE (Strongly Approve)

	Total	Voted Trump	GOP	IND	Mod	Cons
Protecting religious freedom from government interference.	85/15 (54)	90/10 (70)	91/9 (71)	79/21 (44)	81/19 (41)	94/6 (74)
Banning abortions after 20 weeks, or five months of pregnancy, when an unborn child can feel pain.	72/28 (46)	86/14 (62)	83/17 (61)	75/25 (41)	72/28 (38)	86/14 (64)
Restoring pro-family gender language to congress that would end congress' ban on using words like father, mother, son, daughter, brother, sister, husband, and wife.	66/34 (41)	75/25 (60)	79/21 (63)	55/45 (29)	63/37 (26)	75/25 (64)
Appointing conservative Supreme Court Judges.	63/37 (31)	86/14 (54)	83/17 (54)	60/40 (22)	58/42 (14)	87/13 (61)
Mandating a federal ban on taxpayer funded abortions.	56/44 (35)	71/29 (53)	72/28 (50)	50/50 (34)	51/49 (24)	74/26 (57)
Promoting transgenderism in public schools, starting in elementary school.	40/60 (14)	20/80 (6)	23/76 (9)	36/65 (8)	42/58 (9)	21/78 (9)

APPROVALS: CHINA

APPROVE/DISAPPROVE (Strongly Approve)

	Total	Voted Trump	GOP	IND	Mod	Cons
Requiring fair trade with communist China to bring back manufacturing jobs from China to America.	82/18 (44)	83/17 (53)	83/17 (52)	80/20 (43)	78/22 (34)	85/15 (59)
Promoting free and democratic elections, and human rights in China	73/27 (33)	66/34 (34)	72/28 (38)	70/30 (26)	69/31 (21)	75/25 (40)

NOTES

INTRODUCTION: THE STRUGGLE CONTINUES

1 https://www.nationalchurchillmuseum.org/never-give-in-never-never-never.html.

2 https://ballotpedia.org/Partisan_composition_of_state_legislatures.

3 https://nypost.com/2021/05/19/chicagos-mayor-refuses-to-give-interviews-to-white-reporters/.

CHAPTER ONE: YOU AIN'T SEEN NOTHING YET

1 https://www.reaganlibrary.gov/archives/speech/address-nation-eve-presidential-election.

2 https://www.pbs.org/wgbh/americanexperience/features/carter-crisis/.

3 https://www.americanrhetoric.com/speeches/ronaldreaganlibertypark.htm.

4 https://www.history.com/this-day-in-history/gorbachev-resigns-as-president-of-the-ussr.

5 https://www.axios.com/pandemic-unemployment-fraud-benefits-stolen-a937ad9d-0973-4aad-814f-4ca47b72f67f.html.

CHAPTER TWO: BIPARTISAN BALONEY

1 https://www.whitehouse.gov/briefing-room/speeches-remarks/2021/01/20/inaugural-address-by-president-joseph-r-biden-jr/.

2 https://today.yougov.com/topics/science/survey-results/daily/2020/11/11/e0b41/3?utm_source=twitter&utm_medium=daily_agenda&utm_campaign=question_3.

3 https://www.bbc.com/news/world-us-canada-30103078.

4 https://www.pewresearch.org/fact-tank/2017/02/21/public-divided-over-keystone-xl-dakota-pipelines-democrats-turn-decisively-against-keystone/.

5 https://news.gallup.com/poll/344252/americans-emphasis-environmental-protection-shrinks.aspx.

6 https://uagetinvolved.org/content/
keystone-xl-decision-will-raise-energy-costs-american-families.

7 https://www.washingtonexaminer.com/opinion/one-year-later-the-world-health-organization-still-hasnt-addressed-its-failures.

8 https://www.pewresearch.org/fact-tank/2020/06/11/americans-views-on-world-health-organization-split-along-partisan-lines-as-trump-calls-for-u-s-to-withdraw/.

9 https://static1.squarespace.com/static/59153bc0e6f2e109b2a85cbc/t/603d4 22ccfad7f5152ab9a40/1614627374630/Populace+Aspirations+Index.pdf.

10 https://www.axios.com/biden-immigration-reform-poll-d4d85b90-07f9-4a7d-b8ea-b18e35365257.html.

11 https://morningconsult.com/2021/02/10/
biden-refugee-cap-executive-orders-polling/.

12 https://www.gingrich360.com/2020/09/25/
revising-revisionism-the-new-york-times-1619-project/.

13 https://www.dailysignal.com/2020/07/29/parents-school-board-members-divided-on-teaching-1619-project-poll-finds/.

14 https://www.cnn.com/interactive/2021/politics/biden-executive-orders/.

15 https://www.stripes.com/news/us/pentagon-rejects-permit-request-by-veterans-group-for-memorial-day-motorcycle-ride-1.672132.

16 https://www.washingtonpost.com/opinions/2020/11/17/
republicans-women-minorities-congress-record/.

CHAPTER THREE: THE MAD DASH FOR POWER

1 https://ourworldindata.org/covid-vaccinations?country=USA.

2 https://www.bls.gov/charts/employment-situation/civilian-unemployment-rate.htm.

3 https://thehill.com/blogs/congress-blog/
politics/541338-hr-1-isnt-for-the-people-its-for-the-politicians?rl=1.

4 https://www.fec.gov/about/leadership-and-structure/.

5 https://www.foxnews.com/politics/
bennie-thompson-only-dem-vote-against-hr1-election-bill.

6 https://www.republicanleader.gov/
the-truth-behind-democrats-election-bill-h-r-1/.

7 https://nationalinterest.org/blog/politics/
joe-bidens-coronavirus-stimulus-bill-19-trillion-disaster-179765.

8 https://www.nationalreview.com/2021/04/
bidens-tax-plan-will-destroy-american-jobs/.

9 https://www.hoover.org/research/giveaways-disguised-infrastructure.

10 https://nypost.com/2021/05/17/
bidens-infrastructure-plan-wages-war-on-the-suburban-dream/.

11 https://apnews.com/article/freedom-of-religion-coronavirus-pandemic-
reno-us-supreme-court-courts-2e9fb11a6aea2b6b57a2aafeb7a64610.

CHAPTER FOUR: HOW WE GOT HERE

1 https://fred.stlouisfed.org/series/MEHOINUSA672N.

2 https://thehill.com/homenews/campaign/302817-government-workers-
shun-trump-give-big-money-to-clinton-campaign.

CHAPTER FIVE: REFORMING TO ENSURE FREE, FAIR, SECURE ELECTIONS

1 https://www.census.gov/library/stories/2021/04/record-high-turnout-in-
2020-general-election.html.

2 https://www.aclu.org/sites/default/files/field_document/aclu_voter_id_
fact_sheet_-_final.pdf.

3 https://www.pewresearch.org/internet/fact-sheet/internet-broadband/.

4 https://www.pewresearch.org/fact-tank/2018/11/15/how-americans-view-
some-of-the-voting-policies-approved-at-the-ballot-box/.

5 https://www.pewtrusts.org/~/media/legacy/uploadedfiles/pcs_assets/2012/
pewupgradingvoterregistrationpdf.pdf.

6 https://www.americanbar.org/groups/crsj/publications/human_rights_
magazine_home/voting-rights/-use-it-or-lose-it---the-problem-of-purges-
from-the-registration/.

7 https://www.ncsl.org/research/elections-and-campaigns/voter-list-accuracy.
aspx.

8 https://www.pewtrusts.org/~/media/legacy/uploadedfiles/pcs_assets/2012/
pewupgradingvoterregistrationpdf.pdf.

9 https://apnews.com/article/donald-trump-california-66ee694e83d047d5ba
d19ed4d8ba0418.

10 https://www.heritage.org/election-integrity/commentary/
vote-harvesting-recipe-coercion-and-election-fraud.

11 https://congressionalresearch.org/SecretBallot.html.

CHAPTER SIX: UNDERSTANDING AND DEFEATING WOKEISM

1 https://hipatiapress.com/hpjournals/index.php/generos/article/view/1683.

2 https://nypost.com/2021/05/08/
disney-goes-woke-with-new-anti-racist-agenda-for-employees/.

3 https://www.entrepreneur.com/article/366132.

4 https://www.dailywire.com/news/leaked-audio-superintendent-tells-
teachers-crt-isnt-optional-anymore-if-youre-not-willing-then-maybe-this-
isnt-the-right-place-for-you.

5 https://www.ama-assn.org/about/leadership/
ama-s-strategic-plan-embed-racial-justice-and-advance-health-equity.

6 https://www.washingtonpost.com/national/states-vaccine-
rollout/2021/02/03/eae671a0-656f-11eb-886d-5264d4ceb46d_story.html.

7 http://bostonreview.net/science-nature-race/
bram-wispelwey-michelle-morse-antiracist-agenda-medicine.

8 https://www.cnn.com/2021/05/15/politics/space-force-lohmeier-fired-after-
comments/index.html.

9 https://www.amazon.com/gp/product/147980276X/
ref=as_li_qf_asin_il_tl?ie=UTF8.

10 https://stanford.library.sydney.edu.au/archives/fall2008/entries/critical-
theory/#:~:text=According%20to%20these%20theorists%2C%20
a,(Horkheimer%201982%2C%20244).

11 https://www.texastribune.org/2021/05/04/
gary-o-connor-oreo-texas-democrats/.

12 https://nypost.com/2021/04/28/
gop-sen-tim-scott-delivers-scathing-rebuttal-on-bidens-speech/.

13 https://www.newsweek.com/twitter-blocks-uncle-tim-trends-after-racist-
phrase-goes-viral-response-tim-scotts-speech-1587456.

14 https://www.foxnews.com/media/
uncle-tim-slur-tim-scott-trends-twitter-biden-rebuttal.

15 https://www.huffpost.com/entry/
nicolle-wallace-tim-scott-fact-check_n_608a3185e4b0ccb91c2dc9b9.

16 https://twitter.com/Acyn/status/1387600035467067396.

17 https://twitter.com/RevJJackson/status/1387610019219312641.

18 https://wdet.org/posts/2021/05/10/90938-breaking-down-sen-tim-scotts-
claim-that-america-is-not-a-racist-country/.

19 https://www.foxnews.com/media/joy-behar-says-tim-scott-doesnt-seem-
to-understand-the-difference-in-a-racist-country-and-systemic-racism.

20 https://www.sierraclub.org/outdoors/2016/12/
unbearable-whiteness-hiking-and-how-solve-it.

21 https://www.nytimes.com/2016/04/10/magazine/the-unbearable-
whiteness-of-baseball.html.

22 https://www.washingtonpost.com/outlook/2019/12/23/
how-star-wars-reinforces-our-prejudices/.

23 https://www.theguardian.com/technology/shortcuts/2019/mar/13/
driverless-cars-racist.

24 https://medium.com/our-human-family/the-grocery-store-can-show-us-
how-systemic-racism-works-a0c40cb610bc.

25 https://pharos.vassarspaces.net/2019/01/25/
western-civilization-means-classics-and-white-supremacy/.

26 https://urnex.com/blog/addressing-anti-blackness-in-specialty-coffee/.

27 https://www.npr.org/sections/deceptivecadence/2019/09/20/762514169/
why-is-american-classical-music-so-white.

28 https://www.bicycling.com/culture/a33471755/talk-about-racism/.

29 https://www.insider.com/why-straight-relationships-are-doomed-
according-to-sex-researcher-2020-12.

30 https://spoonuniversity.com/lifestyle/
the-candy-industry-has-a-long-history-of-racism-that-we-can-t-ignore.

31 https://web.archive.org/web/20151004200336/http://blacklivesmatter.
com/guiding-principles/.

32 https://ewerickson.substack.com/p/tone-deaf-politics-democrats-
erase?fbclid=IwAR0dycZVTPU-Ut63MurGjzmpq8NOyv4HsbT5sHTJz
njZRkB4nACIFt0x59E.

33 https://www.robindiangelo.com/wp-content/uploads/2016/06/Anti-racism-handout-1-page-2016.pdf.

34 Ozlem Sensoy and Robin D'Angelo, Is Everyone Really Equal? An Introduction to Key Concepts in Social Justice, 197.

35 Robin D'Angelo, White Fragility, 149–50.

36 https://bariweiss.substack.com/p/the-psychopathic-problem-of-the-white.

37 https://www.federalregister.gov/documents/2021/04/19/2021-08068/proposed-priorities-american-history-and-civics-education.

38 https://nmaahc.si.edu/learn/talking-about-race/topics/whiteness.

39 https://www.nytimes.com/2020/07/15/magazine/white-fragility-robin-diangelo.html?action=click&module=Editors%20Picks&pgtype=Homepage.

40 https://www.kipp.org/retiring-work-hard-be-nice/.

41 https://reason.com/2021/05/04/california-math-framework-woke-equity-calculus/.

42 https://sites.google.com/scusd.edu/antiracistclassroom/reflect/groups.

43 https://thedispatch.com/p/how-anti-racism-is-derailing-efforts.

44 https://www.foxnews.com/us/oregon-education-math-white-supremacy.

45 https://twitter.com/kamalaharris/status/1322963321994289154.

46 https://www.whitehouse.gov/briefing-room/presidential-actions/2021/01/20/executive-order-advancing-racial-equity-and-support-for-underserved-communities-through-the-federal-government/.

CHAPTER SEVEN: THE MORAL CASE AGAINST WOKEISM

1 https://knightfoundation.org/wp-content/uploads/2020/01/Knight_Foundation_Free_Expression_on_Campus_2017.pdf.

2 https://www.youtube.com/watch?v=4jAD-EuPCsY.

3 https://www.nbcnews.com/news/nbcblk/map-see-which-states-have-passed-critical-race-theory-bills-n1271215.

4 https://www.edweek.org/policy-politics/teachers-appeal-on-peace-speech-denied/2007/10.

5 https://www.1776action.org/candidate-pledge/.

6 http://consumersresearch.org/press-release-consumers-research-launches-initiative-warning-companies-to-put-consumers-first-and-stop-playing-woke-political-games/.

7 https://www.dailysignal.com/2021/04/13/how-far-left-infiltrated-corporate-america-and-what-can-be-done-about-it/.

8 https://www.wsj.com/articles/woke-capitals-political-warning-11612568436.

9 https://www.nytimes.com/2021/02/26/arts/trump-biden-executive-orders-federal-buildings-architecture.html.

CHAPTER EIGHT: FREEDOM, WORK, AND PROPERTY

1 https://constitutioncenter.org/blog/thomas-paine-the-original-publishing-viral-superstar-2.

2 https://www.rasmussenreports.com/public_content/business/jobs_employment/july_2012/83_favor_work_requirement_for_welfare_recipients.

3 https://abc7news.com/california-edd-unemployment-fraud-ca-scam-insurance/10011810/.

4 https://www.axios.com/pandemic-unemployment-fraud-benefits-stolen-a937ad9d-0973-4aad-814f-4ca47b72f67f.html.

CHAPTER NINE: PEACE, SAFETY, AND STABILITY

1 https://www.iii.org/fact-statistic/facts-statistics-civil-disorders.

2 https://www.forbes.com/sites/jemimamcevoy/2020/06/08/14-days-of-protests-19-dead/?sh=446a44774de4.

3 https://www.independent.co.uk/news/world/americas/george-floyd-minneapolis-defund-police-force-b1816599.html.

4 https://www.foxnews.com/us/police-defunded-cities-murders-crime-budget.

5 https://www.policedefense.org/less-policing-more-murders/.

6 https://www.pewresearch.org/politics/2020/07/09/majority-of-public-favors-giving-civilians-the-power-to-sue-police-officers-for-misconduct/.

7 https://www.pewresearch.org/politics/2020/07/09/majority-of-public-favors-giving-civilians-the-power-to-sue-police-officers-for-misconduct/.

8 https://www.nationalreview.com/2019/01/
border-walls-democrat-partisan-politics/.

9 https://www.dhs.gov/news/2018/12/12/walls-work.

10 https://ballotpedia.org/Laws_permitting_noncitizens_
to_vote_in_the_United_States.

11 https://www.cnn.com/interactive/2021/04/politics/
biden-administration-border-crisis/.

12 https://apnews.com/article/joe-biden-media-coronavirus-
pandemic-immigration-ac00c21ef3be0e7d7213461289a
7ba84.

13 https://www.cnn.com/2021/03/22/politics/biden-administration-press-
access-border-facilities/index.html.

14 https://www.axios.com/border-crossing-migrant-surge-decade-number-
immigration-49062627-9605-4724-8628-c3f96bea8567.html.

15 https://nypost.com/2021/03/22/
us-mexico-border-traffickers-earned-as-much-as-14m-a-day-last-month/.

CHAPTER TEN: RENEWING AMERICAN LEADERSHIP

1 https://www.theguardian.com/world/2021/jan/13/china-in-darkest-period-
for-human-rights-since-tiananmen-says-rights-group.

2 https://www.bbc.com/news/world-asia-china-52765838.

3 http://reuters.com/world/asia-pacific/
impact-national-security-law-hong-kong-2021-05-31/.

4 https://www.gingrich360.com/2021/05/22/a-critical-tool-for-advancing-
and-defending-international-religious-freedom/.

5 https://2017-2021.state.gov/determination-of-the-secretary-of-state-on-
atrocities-in-xinjiang/index.html.

6 https://www.reuters.com/article/us-usa-china-concentrationcamps/
china-putting-minority-muslims-in-concentration-camps-us-says-
idUSKCN1S925K.

7 https://www.cfr.org/backgrounder/chinas-repression-uyghurs-xinjiang.

8 https://www.reuters.com/world/us-calls-xinjiang-an-open-air-prison-
decries-religious-persecution-by-china-2021-05-12/.

9 https://www.bbc.com/news/world-asia-china-55794071.

10 https://apnews.com/article/only-on-ap-middle-east-europe-government-and-politics-76acafd6547fb7cc9ef03c0dd0156eab.

11 https://www.aspi.org.au/report/uyghurs-sale.

12 https://www.cbp.gov/trade/programs-administration/forced-labor/withhold-release-orders-and-findings.

13 https://about.bnef.com/blog/global-wind-industry-had-a-record-near-100gw-year-as-ge-goldwind-took-lead-from-vestas/#:~:text=The%20latest%20data%20from%20research,the%202020%20ranking%5B1%5D.

14 https://www.scmp.com/news/china/article/3115771/us-moves-renewable-energy-wind-turbines-xinjiang-may-get-caught#_=_.

15 https://www.nytimes.com/2021/01/08/business/economy/china-solar-companies-forced-labor-xinjiang.html.

16 https://www.congress.gov/bill/116th-congress/senate-bill/1838/actions?q=%7B%22search%22%3A%5B%22hong+kong+human+rights+and+democracy+act+2019%22%5D%7D&r=1&s=2.

17 https://www.congress.gov/bill/116th-congress/senate-bill/3744/actions?q=%7B%22search%22%3A%5B%22uyghur+human+rights+policy+act%22%5D%7D&r=1&s=5.

18 https://www.congress.gov/bill/116th-congress/house-bill/7440.

19 https://www.washingtonpost.com/politics/2021/05/28/daily-202-biden-faces-bipartisan-pressure-chinas-olympics/.

20 https://reschenthaler.house.gov/media/press-releases/reschenthaler-waltz-and-katko-introduce-resolution-urging-boycott-2022-winter.

21 https://waltz.house.gov/news/documentsingle.aspx?DocumentID=504.

22 https://www.rfa.org/english/news/uyghur/boycott-05182021190458.html.

23 https://www.rubio.senate.gov/public/index.cfm/2021/1/rubio-merkley-colleagues-re-introduce-uyghur-forced-labor-prevention-act.

24 https://mcgovern.house.gov/news/documentsingle.aspx?DocumentID=398673.

25 https://news.gallup.com/poll/337457/new-high-perceptions-china-greatest-enemy.aspx.

26 https://www.cnbc.com/2020/01/30/china-trade-deficit-has-cost-us-3point7-million-jobs-this-century-epi-says.html.

27 https://www.statista.com/chart/20858/top-10-countries-by-share-of-global-manufacturing-output/#:~:text=According%20to%20data%20published%20by,China%20overtook%20it%20in%202010.

28 https://fas.org/sgp/crs/row/IF10964.pdf.

29 https://fortune.com/2021/01/18/chinas-2020-gdp-world-no-1-economy-us/#:~:text=China's%20GDP%20will%20grow%205.7,rest%20of%20the%20forecast%20horizon.%22.

30 https://www.cnbc.com/2021/03/26/us-will-remain-richer-than-china-for-the-next-50-years-or-more-eiu.html#:~:text=China%20set%20to%20be%20world's,%2D19%20pandemic%2C%20he%20added.

31 https://www.hsdl.org/?view&did=812268.

32 https://www.newsweek.com/qatar-subsidies-trump-airlines-1448314.

33 https://www.forbes.com/sites/kenrapoza/2021/03/14/how-chinas-solar-industry-is-set-up-to-be-the-new-green-opec/?sh=87f8a131446d.

34 https://twitter.com/joebiden/status/1283186263302918144?lang=en.

35 https://news.yahoo.com/john-kerry-suggest-oil-workers-211114294.html.

36 https://www.forbes.com/sites/kenrapoza/2021/03/14/how-chinas-solar-industry-is-set-up-to-be-the-new-green-opec/?sh=87f8a131446d.

37 https://www.forbes.com/sites/kenrapoza/2021/03/14/how-chinas-solar-industry-is-set-up-to-be-the-new-green-opec/?sh=87f8a131446d.

38 https://www.afpc.org/uploads/documents/Defense_Technology_Briefing_-_Issue_22.pdf.

39 https://www.afpc.org/uploads/documents/Defense_Technology_Briefing_-_Issue_22.pdf.

40 https://www.usitc.gov/publications/332/executive_briefings/ebot_rare_earths_part_1.pdf.

41 https://www.airforcemag.com/article/rare-elements-of-security/.

42 https://www.defense.gov/Newsroom/Releases/Release/Article/2418542/dod-announces-rare-earth-element-awards-to-strengthen-domestic-industrial-base/.

43 https://www.usgs.gov/news/interior-releases-2018-s-final-list-35-minerals-deemed-critical-us-national-security-and.

44 https://pubs.usgs.gov/periodicals/mcs2021/mcs2021.pdf.

45 https://www.ft.com/content/d3ed83f4-19bc-4d16-b510-415749c032c1.

46 https://www.foxbusiness.com/markets/
biden-looks-abroad-electric-vehicle-metals-us-miners.

47 https://www.eia.gov/todayinenergy/detail.php?id=43515.

48 https://www.washingtonpost.com/graphics/2021/climate-environment/
biden-climate-environment-actions/.

49 https://www.foxbusiness.com/energy/keystone-xl-cancellation-has-ripple-
effect-on-pipeline-workers-native-americans.

50 https://www.wsj.com/articles/federal-judge-stops-biden-administration-
from-blocking-new-oil-and-gas-leases-11623794412.

51 https://about.bnef.com/blog/global-wind-industry-had-a-record-near-
100gw-year-as-ge-goldwind-took-lead-from-vestas/#:~:text=The%20latest
%20data%20from%20research,the%202020%20ranking%5B1%5D.

52 https://www.eia.gov/todayinenergy/detail.php?id=43515.

53 https://www.eia.gov/todayinenergy/detail.php?id=46776.

54 https://www.cnn.com/ALLPOLITICS/1996/conventions/san.diego/facts/
GOP.speeches.past/84.kirkpatrick.shtml.

55 https://www.eia.gov/dnav/pet/hist/LeafHandler.
ashx?n=PET&s=EMM_EPM0_PTE_NUS_DPG&f=W.

56 https://republicanleader.house.gov/
rep-garret-graves-what-we-believe-and-why/.

57 https://www.eia.gov/petroleum/gasdiesel/.

58 https://republicanleader.house.gov/
rep-garret-graves-what-we-believe-and-why/.

59 https://www.eia.gov/energyexplained/us-energy-facts/.

60 https://republicanleader.house.gov/
rep-garret-graves-what-we-believe-and-why/.

61 https://republicanleader.house.gov/
rep-garret-graves-what-we-believe-and-why/.

62 https://clearpath.org/our-take/
the-energy-act-of-2020-a-monumental-climate-and-clean-energy-bill/.

63 https://www.republicanleader.gov/the-energy-innovation-agenda/.

64 https://thehill.com/opinion/energy-environment/549449-house-republicans-deliver-a-commonsense-climate-plan.

65 https://www.npr.org/2021/04/16/985439655/a-worst-nightmare-cyberattack-the-untold-story-of-the-solarwinds-hack.

66 https://www.reuters.com/technology/microsoft-says-group-behind-solarwinds-hack-now-targetting-government-agencies-2021-05-28/.

67 https://www.washingtonpost.com/politics/2021/04/26/cybersecurity-202-nearly-two-thirds-cybersecurity-experts-think-biden-response-russian-hack-is-sufficient/.

68 https://blogs.microsoft.com/on-the-issues/2021/05/27/nobelium-cyberattack-nativezone-solarwinds/.

69 https://news.gallup.com/poll/339974/cyberterrorism-tops-list-potential-threats.aspx.

70 https://news.yahoo.com/justice-department-recovers-majority-of-colonial-pipeline-ransom-we-turned-the-tables-on-dark-side-210611828.html.

71 https://www.wsj.com/articles/colonial-pipeline-ceo-tells-why-he-paid-hackers-a-4-4-million-ransom-11621435636.

72 https://www.bbc.com/news/world-us-canada-57338896.

73 https://www.wsj.com/articles/jbs-paid-11-million-to-resolve-ransomware-attack-11623280781.

74 https://www.wsj.com/articles/colonial-pipeline-ceo-tells-why-he-paid-hackers-a-4-4-million-ransom-11621435636.

75 https://www.nbcnews.com/politics/national-security/they-are-hair-fire-biden-admin-mulling-cyber-attacks-against-n1269575.

CHAPTER ELEVEN: AMERICAN SURVIVAL IS AT RISK

1 https://nypost.com/2021/05/07/us-says-it-has-no-plan-to-shoot-down-out-of-control-chinese-rocket/.

2 https://nypost.com/2021/07/05/bagram-airfield-looted-as-us-forces-leave-afghan-base/.

3 https://www.globalsecurity.org/military/systems/ground/tank-history2-4.htm.

4 James E. Hewes, From Root to McNamara: Army Organization and Administration, 1900–1963 (CreateSpace, 2015).

NOTES

5 https://fas.org/issues/nuclear-weapons/status-world-nuclear-forces/.

6 https://www.bbc.com/news/magazine-33678717.

7 https://www.thedailybeast.com/the-mafia-ruling-ukraines-mobs.

8 https://fas.org/sgp/crs/row/R46139.pdf.

9 https://www.aljazeera.com/features/2020/10/1/
what-has-russia-gained-from-five-years-of-fighting-in-syria.

10 https://www.reuters.com/article/syria-security-russia-grains/update-
1-russia-to-invest-500-mln-in-syrian-port-build-grain-hub-interfax-
idUSL8N28R32J.

11 https://pentagontours.osd.mil/Tours/facts.html.

12 https://www.k12academics.com/education-reform/nation-risk#:~:
text=A%20Nation%20at%20Risk%20was,Commission%20on%20
Excellence%20in%20Education.&text=It%20said%2C%20%22If%20
an%20unfriendly,as%20an%20act%20of%20war.